JAMESTOWN EDUCATION

Timed Readings Plus *in Literature*

25 Two-Part Lessons
with Questions for
Building Reading Speed and Comprehension

B O O K 2

D1029394

McGraw Hill **Glencoe**

JAMESTOWN EDUCATION

Image Credits:
Cover (clock) CORBIS, (book and glasses) Brand X/Jupiter Images,
(quill) CORBIS.

The McGraw-Hill Companies

Mc
Graw
Hill
**Macmillan/McGraw-Hill
Glencoe**

Send all inquiries to:
Glencoe/McGraw-Hill
8787 Orion Place
Columbus, OH 43240-4027

ISBN: 978-0-07-879447-6
MHID: 0-07-879447-1

Printed in the United States of America.

2 3 4 5 6 7 8 9 10 021 11 10 09 08

CONTENTS

The purpose of this book is to help you increase your reading rate and help you better understand what you read. The 25 two-part lessons in this book will also give you practice in reading literature passages and help you prepare for tests in which you must read and interpret passages within a certain time limit.

Reading Faster and Better

Why Read Faster?

The quick and simple answer is that faster readers are better readers. Does this statement surprise you? You might think that fast readers miss things, causing their understanding to suffer. This is not true, for two reasons:

1. Faster readers comprehend faster. When you read faster, the author's message comes to you faster. The text makes sense sooner because the ideas connect sooner. The more quickly you can see how the ideas, characters, and events are related to one another, the more quickly you can understand the meaning of what you are reading.

2. Faster readers concentrate better. Concentration is essential for comprehension. If your mind is wandering, you won't understand what you are reading. A lack of concentration causes you to reread, sometimes over and over, in order to understand the material. Faster readers concentrate better because

there's less time for distractions to interfere with their understanding.

Here are some strategies you can use when you read the passages in each lesson.

Previewing

Previewing before you read is a very important step. This helps you to get an idea of what a passage is about and to recall any previous knowledge you have about the subject. Here are the steps to follow when previewing.

Read the title. Titles are designed not only to announce the subject but also to make the reader think. Ask yourself questions, such as, Is the title about a person, a place, or an event? What thoughts does the title bring to mind? What do I already know about this subject? Also read the author's name, and ask yourself, Have I heard this author's name before? Have I ever read anything written by this author?

Read the first sentence or two. The first sentence can give you clues about the topic of the passage. Is the author describing the setting of the story? Is the author trying to convey a certain emotion? Is the author explaining an event or action?

Skim the entire selection. Glance through the selection quickly for information that will help you read fluently and with understanding.

For example, do you see any characters' names? How many characters are there? Does the passage include names of places or specific dates? This information will help you better comprehend the characters, plot, and setting as you read.

Look at the paragraph structure. Glance over the paragraph breaks and punctuation in the passage. Look for quotation marks and paragraph breaks that signal dialogue to determine whether the passage includes a conversation between characters. If the passage includes a conversation, you know that you will need to pay attention to what the characters say to get clues about what they are thinking and feeling.

Reading for Meaning

The author of a work of literature is not trying to teach the reader or present factual information. Rather, the author is trying to please the reader. The author wants to share feelings and experiences with the reader, to reach him or her in a personal way. This is why the language of literature is rich with meaning.

As you practice reading literature, you develop your ability to use the information in the text to connect to the deeper meanings that the author is trying to communicate. These same skills can also be put to work when you are reading textbooks, to help you organize facts into a meaningful body of knowledge.

Here are some ways to make more sense of what you read.

Build your concentration. You cannot understand what you read if you are not concentrating. When you discover that your thoughts are straying, correct the situation right away. Try to avoid distractions and distracting situations. Keep in mind the information you learned from previewing. This will help focus your attention on what you are reading.

Read in thought groups. Try to see meaningful combinations of words—phrases, clauses, or sentences. If you look at only one word at a time (word-by-word reading), both your comprehension and your reading speed suffer.

Ask yourself questions. To sustain the pace you have set for yourself and to maintain a high level of concentration and comprehension, ask yourself questions as you read, such as, What does this action show about the character? or, What emotion do I feel as I read the author's description of this event?

Mastering Reading Comprehension

Part A

Reading fast is not useful if you don't remember or understand what you have read. The 10 questions in Part A provide two ways for you to check how well you understand the text.

Recalling Facts

These five multiple-choice questions provide a quick way to check how well you recall important information from the passage. As you learn to apply the reading strategies described earlier, you should be able to answer these questions more successfully.

Understanding Ideas

These five questions require you to think about the main ideas in the passage. Some main ideas are stated in the passage; others are not. To answer some of the questions, you need to draw conclusions about what you read.

Part B

The five activities in Part B require multiple answers. These exercises provide practice in applying comprehension and critical thinking skills that you can use in all your reading.

Recognizing Words in Context

Always check to see whether the words around an unfamiliar word—its context—can give you a clue to the word's meaning.

Suppose, for example, that you are unsure of the meaning of the word *expired* in the following passage:

> Vera wanted to check out a book, but her library card had expired. She had to borrow my card because she didn't have time to renew hers.

You could begin to figure out the meaning of *expired* by asking yourself a question such as, What could have happened to Vera's library card that would make her need to borrow someone else's card? You might realize that if Vera had to renew her card, its usefulness must have come to an end or run out. This would lead you to conclude that the word *expired* must mean "to come to an end" or "to run out." You would be right. The context suggested the meaning.

Context can also affect the meaning of a word you already know. The word *key,* for instance, has many meanings. There are musical keys, door keys, and keys to solving a mystery. The context in which the word *key* occurs will tell you which meaning is correct.

Sometimes a word is explained by the words that immediately follow it. The subject of a sentence and your knowledge about that subject might also help you determine the meaning of an unknown word. Try to decide the meaning of the word *revive* in the following sentence:

> Sunshine and water will revive those drooping plants.

The compound subject is *sunshine and water.* You know that plants need light and water to survive and that drooping plants are not healthy. You can figure out that *revive* means "to bring back to health."

Keeping Events in Order

Sequence, or chronological order, is the order of events in a story or the order of steps in a process. Paying attention to the sequence of events or steps will help you follow what is happening, predict what might happen next, and make sense of a passage.

To make the sequence as clear as possible, writers often use signal words to help the reader get a more exact idea of when things happen. Following is a list of frequently used signal words and phrases:

until	first
next	then
before	after
finally	later
when	while
during	now
at the end	by the time
as soon as	in the beginning

Signal words and phrases are also useful when a writer chooses to relate details or events out of sequence. You need to pay careful attention to determine the correct chronological order.

Making Evaluations

Evaluating is making judgments or forming opinions about what you are reading and how it is presented. When you evaluate, you are using your personal understanding and ideas to help you understand the story.

To make an evaluation, think about your reaction to what happens in a passage. Consider the way the author presents the characters and information. Ask yourself, What do I think about what I just read? To answer this question, you will need to draw on your prior knowledge and experiences as well as on your personal beliefs and ideas.

Look at the following passage:

Isabel frowned and moaned when the nanny turned away. The six-year-old kicked her shoe, then the sock, off her foot. The nanny sighed and collected the scattered pieces. She was growing more and more weary of Isabel's stubborn behavior.

After reading the passage, you might make the evaluation *Isabel is a spoiled child*. But someone else might make a different evaluation, such as *The nanny does not give Isabel enough attention*. Both evaluations are judgments that are supported by the information in the passage.

It is important to know the difference between an evaluation and a statement that comes directly from the text. A person who reads the passage and says, "The nanny is getting tired," is not making an evaluation. The person is simply restating the information that is already provided in the text without making a judgment or forming an opinion about characters, places, or events that goes beyond the text.

As you read, be aware of the evaluations that you make about characters, places, and events that the author describes.

Making Correct Inferences

Much of what you read *suggests* more than it *says*. Writers often do not state ideas directly in a text. They can't. Think of the time and space it would take to state every idea. And think of how boring that would be! Instead, writers leave it to you, the reader, to fill in the information they leave out—to make inferences. You do this by combining clues in the text with knowledge from your own experience.

You make many inferences every day. Suppose, for example, that you are visiting a friend's house. You see several suitcases near the door. You infer (make an inference) that your neighbor is about to go on a trip. Another day you overhear a conversation. You catch the names of two actors and the words *scene, dialogue,* and *directing.* You infer that the people are discussing a movie or a play.

In these situations and others like them, you infer unstated information from what you observe or read. Readers must make inferences in order to understand text.

Be careful about the inferences you make. One set of facts may suggest several inferences. Some of these inferences could be faulty. A good inference is always supported by sound evidence, or facts and clues that show something to be true.

Remember the suitcases that caused you to infer that your neighbor had plans to travel? That could be a faulty inference. Perhaps your neighbor isn't planning to travel at all. Perhaps the suitcases are there because he or she is going to lend them to a friend. To make a more accurate inference, you would need to look for more evidence.

Summarizing

A summary is a shortened version of a text that includes only the most important ideas in the text. A summary should provide the overall idea of what happens in the passage. A summary does not include any details unnecessary to the overall understanding of the passage. While details are necessary in the story for the reader to enjoy and connect to the story in depth, details are not necessary in a summary.

Look at the following passage and its summary:

Henry and Jordan ran faster and faster. The sound of the train whistle grew sharp in their ears as they approached the station. As the conductor called "All aboard!" in his deep, confident voice, they slipped through the crowd and across the platform and leapt through the closest open door. They had made it! At last they were on their way to Spain.

Summary: *Henry and Jordan run to catch a train to Spain right before it leaves the station.*

This passage describes an event that two characters experience. The summary shown above includes the names of the two characters, what they do, and why they do it. The details about the conductor's voice and the train whistle, for example, are not included in the summary.

As you read the following passage, try to find the most important ideas. Then review the summary.

> The sun shone brightly over the meadow and soon burned off the morning haze. I watched anxiously as Latricia rode faster and faster over the ground, her horse's hooves throwing up clumps of loose sod into the damp air. Latricia's hair flew behind her in a constant wave, as if to bid me good day. They approached the first jump, and I held my breath.

Summary: *The narrator watches anxiously as Latricia rides her horse across the meadow toward the first jump.*

Notice how the summary includes the characters, what they do, and how the narrator feels. It does not include details about how the horse runs or the way Latricia's hair moves. These details are not necessary for understanding the most important ideas in the passage.

Knowing how to summarize is an important skill. It can help you check your understanding as you read and remember the most important parts of the story.

Working Through a Lesson

Part A

1. **Preview the passage.** Locate the timed selection in Part A of the lesson that you are going to read. Wait for your teacher's signal to preview. You will have 20 seconds for previewing. Follow the previewing steps described on pages 2 and 3.

2. **Read the passage.** When your teacher gives you the signal, begin reading. Read carefully so that you will be able to answer questions about what you have read. Your teacher will be writing times on the chalkboard. When you finish reading, look at the chalkboard and note your reading time. Write this time at the bottom of the page on the line labeled Reading Time.

3. **Complete the exercises.** Answer the 10 questions that follow the passage. There are five fact questions and five idea questions. Put an *X* in the box next to the best answer for each question.

4. **Correct your work.** Use the Answer Key at the back of the book to check your answers. Circle any wrong answer and put an *X* in the box you should have marked. Record the number of your correct answers for Part A in the space provided on the last page of the lesson.

Part B

1. **Preview and read the passage.** Use the same techniques you use to read Part A. Think carefully about the meaning of the passage.

2. **Complete the exercises.** There are five activities that help you practice five different skills. Instructions are given for completing each activity. Each activity has three responses, so there are 15 total responses for you to record in Part B.

3. **Correct your work.** Use the Answer Key at the back of the book. Circle any wrong answer and write the correct letter or number next to it. Record the number of your correct answers for Part B in the space provided on the last page of the lesson.

Plotting Your Progress

1. **Find your reading rate.** Turn to the Reading Rate graph on page 116. Put an *X* at the point where the vertical line that represents the lesson intersects your reading time, shown along the left-hand side. The right-hand side of the graph will reveal your words-per-minute reading speed.

2. **Find your comprehension score.** Add your scores for Part A and Part B to determine the total number of your correct answers. Turn to the Comprehension Score Graph on page 117. Put an *X* at the point where the vertical line that represents your lesson intersects your total correct answers, shown along the left-hand side. The right-hand side of the graph will show the percentage of questions you answered correctly.

3. **Complete the Comprehension Skills Profile.** Turn to page 118. Record your incorrect answers for the Part B exercises. The five Part B skills are listed along the bottom. There are five columns of boxes—one column for each question. For every incorrect answer, put an *X* in a box for that skill.

To get the most benefit from these lessons, you need to take charge of your own progress in improving your reading speed and comprehension. Studying these graphs will help you to see whether your reading rate is increasing and to determine what skills you need to work on. Your teacher will also review the graphs to check your progress.

About the Series

Timed Readings Plus in Literature includes 10 books at reading levels 4–13, with one book at each level. Book One contains material at a fourth-grade reading level, Book Two at a fifth-grade level, and so on. The readability level is determined by the Fry Readability Scale and is not to be confused with grade level or age. The books are designed for use with students at middle school level and above.

The purposes of the series are

- to provide systematic, structured reading practice that helps students improve their reading rate and comprehension skills;

- to give students experience in reading literature;

- to prepare students for taking standardized tests that include timed reading passages;

- to provide materials with a wide range of reading levels so that students can continue to practice and improve their reading rate and comprehension skills.

Each book in the series contains 25 two-part lessons. Part A focuses on improving reading rate. This section of the lesson consists of a 400-word timed literature passage followed by two multiple-choice exercises. Recalling Facts includes five fact questions; Understanding Ideas includes five critical thinking questions.

Part B concentrates on building mastery in critical areas of comprehension. This section consists of a non-timed passage—the "plus" passage—followed by five exercises that address five major comprehension skills. The passage varies in length but is generally about 200 words long.

Timed Reading and Comprehension

Timed reading is the best-known method of improving reading speed. However, there is no point in having a student read at an accelerated speed if the student does not understand what she or he is reading. Nothing is more important than comprehension in reading.

Few students will be able to read a passage once and answer all of the questions correctly. A score of 70 or 80 percent correct is standard. If a student gets 90 or 100 percent correct, either he or she is reading too slowly or the material is at too low a reading level. A comprehension or critical thinking score of less than 70 percent indicates a need for improvement.

One method of improving comprehension and critical thinking skills is for the student to go back and study each incorrect answer. First the student should reread the question carefully. Many students choose the wrong answer simply because they have not read the question carefully. Then the student should look back in the passage to find the place where the question is answered, reread that part of the passage, and think about how to arrive at the correct answer. It is important to be able to recognize the correct answer when it is embedded in the text. Teacher guidance or class discussion will help the student find the answer.

Speed Versus Comprehension

It is not unusual for comprehension scores to decline as reading rate increases during the early weeks of timed readings. If this happens, students should attempt to level off their speed—but not lower it—and concentrate more on comprehension. Usually, if students maintain the higher speed and concentrate on comprehension, scores will gradually improve and within a week or two be back up to levels of 70 to 80 percent.

It is important to achieve a proper balance between speed and comprehension. An inefficient reader typically reads everything at one speed, usually slowly. Some poor readers, however, read rapidly but without satisfactory comprehension. It is important to achieve a balance between speed and comprehension. The practice that this series provides enables students to increase their reading speed while maintaining standard levels of comprehension.

Getting Started

Begin by assigning students to a level. A student should start with a book that is one level below his or her current reading level. If a student's reading level is not known, a suitable starting point would be one or two levels below the student's present grade in school.

Introduce students to the contents and format of the book they are using. Examine the book to see how it is organized. Talk about the parts of each lesson. Discuss the purpose of timed reading and the use of the progress graphs at the back of the book.

Timing the Reading

One suggestion for timing the reading is to have all students begin reading the selection at the same time. After one minute, write on the board the time that has elapsed and begin updating it at 10-second intervals (1:00, 1:10, 1:20, etc.). Another option is to have individual students time themselves with a stopwatch.

Teaching a Lesson

Part A

1. Give students the signal to begin previewing the lesson. Allow 20 seconds.

2. Use one of the methods described above to time students as they read the passage. (Include the 20-second preview time as part of the first minute.) Tell students to write down the last time shown on the board or the stopwatch when they finish reading. Have them record the time in the designated space after the passage.

3. Have students complete the exercises in Part A. Work with them to check their answers, using the Answer Key, which begins on page 114. Have them circle incorrect answers, mark the correct answers, and then record the number of correct answers for Part A on the appropriate line at the end of the lesson. Correct responses to eight or more questions indicate satisfactory comprehension and recall.

Part B

1. Have students read the Part B passage and complete the exercises that follow it. Directions are provided with each exercise. Correct responses require deliberation and discrimination.

2. Work with students to check their answers. Then discuss the answers with them and have them record the number of correct answers for Part B at the end of the lesson.

3. Have students study the correct answers to the questions they answered incorrectly. It is important that they understand why a particular answer is correct or incorrect. Have them reread relevant parts of a passage to clarify an answer. An effective cooperative activity is to have students work in pairs to discuss their answers, explain why they chose the answers they did, and try to resolve differences.

Monitoring Progress

Have students find their total correct answers for the lesson and record their reading time and scores on the graphs on pages 116 and 117. Then have them complete the Comprehension Skills Profile on page 118. For each incorrect response to a question in Part B, students should mark an X in the box above each question type.

The legend on the Reading Rate graph automatically converts reading times to words-per-minute rates. The Comprehension Score graph automatically converts the raw scores to percentages.

These graphs provide a visual record of a student's progress. This record gives the student and you an opportunity to evaluate the student's progress and to determine the types of exercises and skills he or she needs to concentrate on.

Diagnosis and Evaluation

The following are typical reading rates:

Slow Reader—150 Words Per
Minute

Average Reader—250 Words Per
Minute

Fast Reader—350 Words Per
Minute

A student who consistently reads at an average or above-average rate (with satisfactory comprehension) is ready to advance to the next book in the series.

A column of *X*'s in the Comprehension Skills Profile indicates a specific comprehension weakness. Using the profile, you can assess trends in student performance and suggest remedial work if necessary.

from **The Strange Case of Dr. Jekyll and Mr. Hyde**

by Robert Louis Stevenson

Mr. Utterson was sitting by his fireside one evening after dinner, when he was surprised to receive a visit from Poole.

"Bless me, Poole, what brings you here?" he cried; and then taking a second look at him, "What ails you?" he added. "Is the doctor ill?"

"Mr. Utterson," said the man, "there is something wrong."

"Take a seat, and here is a glass of wine for you," said the lawyer. "Now, take your time, and tell me plainly what you want."

"You know the doctor's ways, sir," replied Poole, "and how he shuts himself up. Well, he's shut up again in the cabinet. I don't like it, sir—I wish I may die if I like it. Mr. Utterson, sir, I'm afraid."

"Now, my good man," said the lawyer, "be explicit. What are you afraid of?"

"I've been afraid for about a week," returned Poole, doggedly disregarding the question, "and I can bear it no more."

The man's appearance amply bore out his words. His manner was altered for the worse; and except for the moment when he had first announced his terror, he had not once looked the lawyer in the face. Even now, he sat with the glass of wine untasted on his knee, and his eyes directed to a corner of the floor. "I can bear it no more," he repeated.

"Come," said the lawyer, "I see you have some good reason, Poole. I see there is something seriously amiss. Try to tell me what it is."

"I think there's been foul play," said Poole, hoarsely.

"Foul play!" cried the lawyer, a good deal frightened. "What foul play! What does the man mean?"

"I daren't say, sir," was the answer; "but will you come along with me and see for yourself?"

Mr. Utterson's only answer was to rise and get his hat and greatcoat; but he observed with wonder the greatness of the relief that appeared upon the butler's face, and perhaps with no less, that the wine was still untasted when he set it down to follow.

It was a wild, cold night of March, with a pale moon, lying on her back as though the wind had tilted her. The wind made talking difficult, and flecked the blood into the face. It seemed to have swept the streets unusually bare of passengers.

Reading Time _____

Recalling Facts

1. Mr. Utterson offers Poole a glass of
   - ❏ a. brandy.
   - ❏ b. wine.
   - ❏ c. water.

2. The doctor has locked himself in the
   - ❏ a. attic.
   - ❏ b. basement.
   - ❏ c. cabinet.

3. Poole tells Mr. Utterson that he has been afraid for about a
   - ❏ a. day.
   - ❏ b. week.
   - ❏ c. year.

4. Poole thinks there has been
   - ❏ a. foul play.
   - ❏ b. a suicide.
   - ❏ c. a party.

5. This scene takes place on a
   - ❏ a. hot summer evening.
   - ❏ b. windy autumn afternoon.
   - ❏ c. cold March night.

Understanding the Passage

6. Poole apparently works for the
   - ❏ a. doctor.
   - ❏ b. butler.
   - ❏ c. lawyer.

7. Mr. Utterson is familiar with
   - ❏ a. the doctor's strange habits.
   - ❏ b. everyone in town.
   - ❏ c. the butler's fears.

8. Mr. Utterson is surprised that Poole
   - ❏ a. doesn't touch his drink.
   - ❏ b. knew where to find him.
   - ❏ c. left the doctor's side.

9. Poole is happy that
   - ❏ a. the doctor is locked up.
   - ❏ b. Mr. Utterson agrees to come with him.
   - ❏ c. there are no people on the streets.

10. Poole's frame of mind can best be described as
    - ❏ a. desperate.
    - ❏ b. amused.
    - ❏ c. bored.

1 B *from* **The Adventures of Tom Sawyer**
by Mark Twain

Tom's mind was made up now. He was gloomy and desperate. He was a forsaken, friendless boy, he said. Nobody loved him. When they found out what they had driven him to, perhaps they would be sorry. He had tried to do right and get along, but they would not let him. Since nothing would do them but to be rid of him, let it be so. Let them blame *him* for the consequences—why shouldn't they? What right had the friendless to complain? Yes, they had forced him to it at last. He would lead a life of crime. There was no choice.

By this time he was far down Meadow Lane, and the bell for school to "take up" tinkled faintly upon his ear. He sobbed, now, to think he should never, never hear that old familiar sound anymore. It was very hard, but it was forced on him. Since he was driven out into the cold world, he must submit—but he forgave them. Then the sobs came thick and fast.

Just at this point he met his soul's sworn comrade, Joe Harper—hard eyed, and with evidently a great and dismal purpose in his heart. Plainly here were "two souls with but a single thought." Tom began to blubber out something about a resolution to escape home by roaming abroad into the great world never to return; and ended by hoping that Joe would not forget him.

1. **Recognizing Words in Context**

    Find the word *comrade* in the passage. One definition below is closest to the meaning of that word. One definition has the opposite or nearly the opposite meaning. The remaining definition has a completely different meaning. Label each definition C for *closest,* O for *opposite or nearly opposite,* or D for *different.*

    _____ a. friend

    _____ b. teacher

    _____ c. enemy

2. **Keeping Events in Order**

    Number each statement below 1, 2, or 3 to show the order in which the events took place.

    _____ a. Tom hears the bell for school to "take up."

    _____ b. Tom sees Joe Harper on Meadow Lane.

    _____ c. Tom makes up his mind to lead a life of crime.

3. Making Evaluations

Two of the statements below describe things that actually happen or are stated in the passage. The other statement is an evaluation, or a judgment or opinion, about a character, setting, or event in the passage. Label each statement E for *evaluation* or H for *happens or is stated in the passage.*

_____ a. Tom believes that no one loves him.

_____ b. Tom's decision to run away is foolish.

_____ c. Tom cries at the thought that he will never hear the bell again.

4. Making Correct Inferences

Two of the statements below are correct inferences, or reasonable guesses. They are based on information in the passage. The other statement is an incorrect, or faulty, inference. Label each statement C for *correct* inference or F for *faulty* inference.

_____ a. Tom feels unable to succeed in school.

_____ b. Tom's belief that he is friendless is untrue.

_____ c. Tom truly likes his life despite his current feelings.

5. Summarizing

One of the statements below is a summary that tells the most important ideas in the passage. The other two statements contain details from the passage. They do not tell the most important ideas in the passage. Label each statement S for *summary* or D for *details.*

_____ a. Tom tells Joe that he hopes Joe will not forget him when he's gone.

_____ b. Tom cries because he thinks he'll never hear the school bell again.

_____ c. Tom decides to leave home because he thinks no one cares about him.

Correct Answers, Part A _____

Correct Answers, Part B _____

Total Correct Answers _____

from **An Old-Fashioned Girl**
by Louisa May Alcott

"What were you thinking about just now, when you sat staring at the fire?" asked Tom.

"I was thinking about Jimmy," Polly said.

"Would you mind telling about him? You know, you said you would some time; but don't, if you'd rather not," said Tom, lowering his rough voice respectfully.

"I like to talk about him; but there isn't much to tell," began Polly, grateful for his interest. "Sitting here with you reminded me of the way I used to sit with him when he was sick. We used to have such happy times, and it's so pleasant to think about them now."

"He was awfully good, wasn't he?"

"No, he wasn't. But he tried to be, and mother says that is half the battle. We used to get tired of trying; but we kept making resolutions, and working hard to keep 'em. I don't think I got on much; but Jimmy did, and everyone loved him."

"Didn't you ever squabble, as we do?"

"Yes, indeed, sometimes; but we couldn't stay mad, and always made it up again as soon as we could. Jimmy used to come round first, and say, 'All serene, Polly,' so kind and jolly, that I couldn't help laughing and being friends right away."

"Did he not know a lot?"

"Yes, I think he did, for he liked to study, and wanted to get on, so he could help father. People used to call him a fine boy, and I felt so proud to hear it; but they didn't know half how wise he was, because he didn't show off a bit. I suppose sisters always think their brothers are grand. But I don't believe many girls had as much right to be as I had."

"Most girls don't care two pins about their brothers; so that shows you don't know much about it."

"Well, they ought to, if they don't; and they would if the boys were as kind to them as Jimmy was to me."

"Why, what did he do?"

"Loved me dearly, and wasn't ashamed to show it," cried Polly, with a sob in her voice.

"What made him die, Polly?" asked Tom, soberly, after a little pause.

"He got hurt coasting, last winter; but he never told which boy did it, and he only lived a week. I helped take care of him; and he was so patient."

Reading Time _____

Recalling Facts

1. Polly says that she is thinking about
   - ❏ a. Tom.
   - ❏ b. Jimmy.
   - ❏ c. her mother.

2. Polly says that everyone loved
   - ❏ a. her.
   - ❏ b. Tom.
   - ❏ c. Jimmy.

3. Jimmy liked to
   - ❏ a. study.
   - ❏ b. cause trouble.
   - ❏ c. show off.

4. Jimmy was Polly's
   - ❏ a. neighbor.
   - ❏ b. cousin.
   - ❏ c. brother.

5. Jimmy was hurt while
   - ❏ a. coasting.
   - ❏ b. bicycling.
   - ❏ c. hunting.

Understanding the Passage

6. Tom is curious about
   - ❏ a. Jimmy's life.
   - ❏ b. Polly's friends.
   - ❏ c. unusual diseases.

7. Jimmy sometimes
   - ❏ a. broke the law.
   - ❏ b. fought with Polly.
   - ❏ c. both a and b.

8. Jimmy seemed to be
   - ❏ a. arrogant.
   - ❏ b. sincere.
   - ❏ c. greedy.

9. Polly feels that people didn't know just how
   - ❏ a. funny Jimmy could be.
   - ❏ b. smart Jimmy was.
   - ❏ c. dishonest Jimmy was.

10. Polly feels that her relationship with Jimmy was
    - ❏ a. unloving.
    - ❏ b. special.
    - ❏ c. boring.

from **Black Beauty**

by Anna Sewell

Into this fine box the groom put me; it was clean, sweet, and airy. I never was in a better box than that, and the sides were not so high but that I could see all that went on through the iron rails that were at the top.

He gave me some very nice oats, he patted me, spoke kindly, and then went away.

When I had eaten my corn I looked round. In the stall next to mine stood a little fat gray pony, with a thick mane and tail, a very pretty head, and a pert little nose.

I put my head up to the iron rails at the top of my box, and said, "How do you do? What is your name?"

He turned round as far as his halter would allow, held up his head, and said, "My name is Merrylegs. I am very handsome; I carry the young ladies on my back, and sometimes I take our mistress out in the low chair. They think a great deal of me, and so does James. Are you going to live next door to me in the box?"

I said, "Yes."

"Well, then," he said, "I hope you are good tempered; I do not like anyone next door who bites."

1. **Recognizing Words in Context**

   Find the word *pert* in the passage. One definition below is closest to the meaning of that word. One definition has the opposite or nearly the opposite meaning. The remaining definition has a completely different meaning. Label each definition C for *closest*, O for *opposite or nearly opposite*, or D for *different*.

   _____ a. ugly

   _____ b. perky

   _____ c. droopy

2. **Keeping Events in Order**

   Number each statement below 1, 2, or 3 to show the order in which the events took place.

   _____ a. Black Beauty enters his new box.

   _____ b. Merrylegs introduces himself to Black Beauty.

   _____ c. The groom gives Black Beauty some oats.

3. Making Evaluations

Two of the statements below describe things that actually happen or are stated in the passage. The other statement is an evaluation, or a judgment or opinion, about a character, setting, or event in the passage. Label each statement E for *evaluation* or H for *happens or is stated in the passage.*

_____ a. Merrylegs is very proud.

_____ b. Merrylegs has a very pretty head.

_____ c. Black Beauty has never had a better box.

4. Making Correct Inferences

Two of the statements below are correct inferences, or reasonable guesses. They are based on information in the passage. The other statement is an incorrect, or faulty, inference. Label each statement C for *correct* inference or F for *faulty* inference.

_____ a. The same master owns both Black Beauty and Merrylegs.

_____ b. In the past, Merrylegs has had a neighbor who bit.

_____ c. Black Beauty feels jealous of Merrylegs's good looks.

5. Summarizing

One of the statements below is a summary that tells the most important ideas in the passage. The other two statements contain details from the passage. They do not tell the most important ideas in the passage. Label each statement S for *summary* or D for *details.*

_____ a. Black Beauty is put into a nice new stall and meets his new neighbor.

_____ b. Black Beauty likes his new box since he can see out over the sides.

_____ c. Merrylegs carries young ladies on his back and takes the mistress out in a chair.

Correct Answers, Part A _____

Correct Answers, Part B _____

Total Correct Answers _____

3　A　*from* **Vanity Fair**
by William Makepeace Thackeray

Sir Pitt started when he saw poor Rawdon in his study in tumbled clothes, with bloodshot eyes, and his hair over his face. Sir Pitt thought his brother was not sober, and had been out all night on some orgy. "Good gracious, Rawdon," he said, with a blank face, "what brings you here at this time of the morning? Why ain't you at home?"

"Home," said Rawdon, with a wild laugh. "Don't be frightened, Pitt. I'm not drunk. Shut the door; I want to speak to you."

Pitt closed the door and came up to the table, where he seated himself in the other armchair—the one placed for the reception of the steward, agent, or confidential visitor who came to transact business with the Baronet—and trimmed his nails more vehemently than ever.

"Pitt, it's all over with me," the Colonel said, after a pause. "I'm done."

"I always said it would come to this," the Baronet cried peevishly, and beating a tune with his clean-trimmed nails. "I warned you a thousand times. I can't help you any more. Every shilling of my money is tied up. Even the hundred pounds that Jane took you last night were promised to my lawyer tomorrow morning, and the want of it will put me to great inconvenience. I don't mean to say that I won't assist you ultimately. But as for paying your creditors in full, I might as well hope to pay the National debt. It is madness, sheer madness, to think of such a thing. You must come to a compromise. It's a painful thing for the family; but everybody does it. There was George Kitely, Lord Ragland's son, went through the Court last week, and was what they call whitewashed, I believe. Lord Ragland would not pay a shilling for him, and—"

"It's not money I want," Rawdon broke in. "I'm not come to you about myself. Never mind what happens to me—"

"What is the matter, then?" said Pitt, somewhat relieved.

"It's the boy," said Rawdon, in a husky voice. "I want you to promise me that you will take charge of him when I'm gone. That dear good wife of yours has always been good to him, and he's fonder of her than he is of his . . . damn it. Look here, Pitt: you know that I was to have had Miss Crawley's money."

Recalling Facts

1. Sir Pitt is Rawdon's
   - ❏ a. business partner.
   - ❏ b. drinking partner.
   - ❏ c. brother.

2. Rawdon's military rank is
   - ❏ a. lieutenant.
   - ❏ b. captain.
   - ❏ c. colonel.

3. While Rawdon talks, Pitt
   - ❏ a. paces the room.
   - ❏ b. trims his nails.
   - ❏ c. leaves the room.

4. The hundred pounds given to Rawdon had been
   - ❏ a. promised to Pitt's lawyer.
   - ❏ b. set aside for Jane's education.
   - ❏ c. due him for a long time.

5. Rawdon says his real concern is
   - ❏ a. for the boy.
   - ❏ b. getting his creditors paid off.
   - ❏ c. to help his troubled wife.

Understanding the Passage

6. When Pitt first sees Rawdon, he thinks he is
   - ❏ a. dying.
   - ❏ b. drunk.
   - ❏ c. celebrating.

7. Pitt apparently
   - ❏ a. often finds Rawdon in trouble.
   - ❏ b. wants to help Rawdon any way he can.
   - ❏ c. is responsible for Rawdon's problems.

8. Pitt thinks that Rawdon should
   - ❏ a. pay off his creditors in full.
   - ❏ b. turn himself in to the police.
   - ❏ c. strike a deal to pay off some of his debts.

9. Pitt is relieved when Rawdon
   - ❏ a. asks for only a little money.
   - ❏ b. asks for Miss Crawley's money.
   - ❏ c. says he is not asking for money.

10. The boy mentioned in the passage appears to be
    - ❏ a. Pitt's son.
    - ❏ b. Rawdon's son.
    - ❏ c. Pitt's younger brother.

from The Wind in the Willows

by Kenneth Grahame

Rat and Mole waited for what seemed a very long time, stamping in the snow to keep their feet warm. At last they heard the sound of slow shuffling footsteps approaching the door from the inside. It seemed, as the Mole remarked to the Rat, like someone walking in carpet slippers that were too large for him and down-at-heel. This was intelligent of Mole, because that was exactly what it was.

There was the noise of a bolt shot back, and the door opened a few inches, enough to show a long snout and a pair of sleepy blinking eyes.

"Now, the *very* next time this happens," said a gruff voice, "I shall be most angry. Who is it *this* time, disturbing people on such a night? Speak up!"

"O, Badger," cried the Rat, "let us in, please. It's me, Rat, and my friend Mole. We've lost our way in the snow."

"What, Ratty, my dear little man!" exclaimed the Badger, in quite a different voice. "Come along in, both of you, at once. Why, you must be perished. Well I never! Lost in the snow! And in the Wild Wood, too, and at this time of night! But come in with you."

1. **Recognizing Words in Context**

   Find the word *gruff* in the passage. One definition below is closest to the meaning of that word. One definition has the opposite or nearly the opposite meaning. The remaining definition has a completely different meaning. Label each definition C for *closest*, O for *opposite or nearly opposite*, or D for *different.*

   _____ a. rough

   _____ b. smooth

   _____ c. quiet

2. **Keeping Events in Order**

   Number each statement below 1, 2, or 3 to show the order in which the events took place.

   _____ a. Badger invites Rat and Mole into his home.

   _____ b. Rat and Mole hear shuffling footsteps.

   _____ c. Rat and Mole stamp in the snow to keep their feet warm.

3. Making Evaluations

Two of the statements below describe things that actually happen or are stated in the passage. The other statement is an evaluation, or a judgment or opinion, about a character, setting, or event in the passage. Label each statement E for *evaluation* or H for *happens or is stated in the passage.*

_____ a. Mole makes an intelligent remark.

_____ b. Rat and Mole have lost their way.

_____ c. Badger becomes grumpy easily.

4. Making Correct Inferences

Two of the statements below are correct inferences, or reasonable guesses. They are based on information in the passage. The other statement is an incorrect, or faulty, inference. Label each statement C for *correct* inference or F for *faulty* inference.

_____ a. Rat and Badger already know each other.

_____ b. This story takes place late at night.

_____ c. Rat and Mole live in the Wild Wood.

5. Summarizing

One of the statements below is a summary that tells the most important ideas in the passage. The other two statements contain details from the passage. They do not tell the most important ideas in the passage. Label each statement S for *summary* or D for *details.*

_____ a. Mole correctly guesses that the noise is someone walking in slippers.

_____ b. Rat and Mole are lost, and Badger invites them into his home.

_____ c. Rat and Mole see a long snout and a pair of sleepy eyes.

Correct Answers, Part A _____

Correct Answers, Part B _____

Total Correct Answers _____

from The Rocking-Horse Winner

by D. H. Lawrence

The family consisted of a mother, a father, a boy, and two little girls. They lived in a nice house with a garden. They had discreet servants and felt themselves superior to anyone in the neighborhood.

Although they lived in style, they felt always an anxiety in the house. There was never enough money. The mother had a small income, and the father had a small income, but not nearly enough for the social position which they had to keep up. The father went into town to some office. But though he had good prospects, these prospects never came to a thing. There was always the grinding sense of the shortage of money, though the style was always kept up.

At last the mother said, "I will see if *I* can't make something." But she did not know where to begin. She racked her brains. She tried this thing and the other, but could not find anything successful. The failure made deep lines come into her face. Her children were growing up. They would have to go to school. There must be more money, there must be more money. The father, who was always very handsome and expensive in his tastes, seemed as if he never *would* be able to do anything worth doing. And the mother, who had a great belief in herself, did not succeed any better, and her tastes were just as expensive.

And so the house came to be haunted by the unspoken phrase: *There must be more money! There must be more money!* The children could hear it all the time, though nobody said it aloud. They heard it at Christmas, when the expensive and splendid toys filled the nursery. Behind the shining modern rocking horse, behind the smart dollhouse, a voice would start whispering: "There *must* be more money! There *must* be more money!" And the children would stop playing, to listen for a moment. They would look into each other's eyes, to see if they had all heard. And each one saw in the eyes of the other two that they too had heard. "There *must* be more money! There *must* be more money!"

Yet nobody ever said it aloud. The whisper was everywhere, and therefore no one spoke it. Just as no one ever says: "We are breathing!" in spite of the fact that breath is coming and going all the time.

Reading Time _____

Recalling Facts

1. The family lives in a house with
   - ❏ a. a garden.
   - ❏ b. two other families.
   - ❏ c. red shutters.

2. The father has
   - ❏ a. no income.
   - ❏ b. a small income.
   - ❏ c. a large income.

3. The mother has
   - ❏ a. inherited a large sum of money.
   - ❏ b. no love for material objects.
   - ❏ c. expensive tastes.

4. The house is always filled with
   - ❏ a. friends.
   - ❏ b. music.
   - ❏ c. anxiety.

5. The mother's attempts to make more money
   - ❏ a. anger the father.
   - ❏ b. double their savings.
   - ❏ c. do not succeed.

Understanding the Passage

6. The parents insist on
   - ❏ a. keeping up the appearance of wealth.
   - ❏ b. sending their children to live with their grandparents.
   - ❏ c. putting their children to work.

7. At Christmastime, the children receive
   - ❏ a. no presents.
   - ❏ b. a few inexpensive presents.
   - ❏ c. beautiful and expensive presents.

8. The phrase "There *must* be more money!" is heard
   - ❏ a. by no one.
   - ❏ b. only by the boy.
   - ❏ c. by the entire family.

9. The mother has no idea
   - ❏ a. how to make more money.
   - ❏ b. where the father works.
   - ❏ c. why her children are always crying.

10. The father is not
    - ❏ a. well educated.
    - ❏ b. concerned about what other people think.
    - ❏ c. very successful in his job.

from **Life of Ma Parker**
by Katherine Mansfield

When that family moved on she went as "help" to a doctor's house. After two years there, on the run from morning till night, she married her husband. He was a baker.

"A baker, Mrs. Parker!" the literary gentleman said. "It must have been rather nice to be married to a baker!"

Mrs. Parker didn't look so sure.

"Such a clean trade," said the gentleman.

Mrs. Parker didn't look convinced.

"And didn't you like handing the new loaves to the customers?"

"Well, sir," said Mrs. Parker, "I wasn't in the shop above a great deal. We had thirteen little ones and buried seven of them. If it wasn't the hospital it was the infirmary, you might say!"

"You might, *indeed*, Mrs. Parker!" said the gentleman, shuddering.

Yes, seven had gone, and while the six were still small her husband was taken ill with consumption. It was flour on the lungs, the doctor told her at the time. Her husband sat up in bed with his shirt pulled over his head, and the doctor's finger drew a circle on his back.

"Now, if we were to cut him open *here*, Mrs. Parker," said the doctor, "you'd find his lungs chock-a-block with white powder. Breathe, my good fellow!"

1. **Recognizing Words in Context**

   Find the word *consumption* in the passage. One definition below is closest to the meaning of that word. One definition has the opposite or nearly the opposite meaning. The remaining definition has a completely different meaning. Label the definitions C for *closest*, O for *opposite or nearly opposite*, and D for *different*.

   _____ a. health

   _____ b. disease

   _____ c. fear

2. **Keeping Events in Order**

   Number each statement below 1, 2, or 3 to show the order in which the events took place.

   _____ a. The doctor draws a circle with his finger on the husband's back.

   _____ b. Mrs. Parker goes to work as "help" in a doctor's house.

   _____ c. Mrs. Parker marries a baker.

3. Making Evaluations

Two of the statements below describe things that actually happen or are stated in the passage. The other statement is an evaluation, or a judgment or opinion, about a character, setting, or event in the passage. Label each statement E for *evaluation* or H for *happens or is stated in the passage.*

_____ a. Mrs. Parker does not look convinced by the gentleman's remarks.

_____ b. Mrs. Parker has had great misfortune in her life.

_____ c. The literary gentleman says that baking is a clean trade.

4. Making Correct Inferences

Two of the statements below are correct inferences, or reasonable guesses. They are based on information in the passage. The other statement is an incorrect, or faulty, inference. Label each statement C for *correct* inference or F for *faulty* inference.

_____ a. Mrs. Parker's work at the doctor's house was demanding.

_____ b. Mrs. Parker disliked spending time in her husband's shop.

_____ c. Mrs. Parker's husband is no longer alive.

5. Summarizing

One of the statements below is a summary that tells the most important ideas in the passage. The other two statements contain details from the passage. They do not tell the most important ideas in the passage. Label each statement S for *summary* or D for *details.*

_____ a. Mrs. Parker describes hardships in her life to a literary gentleman.

_____ b. The literary gentleman says that being married to a baker must have been nice.

_____ c. The doctor told Mrs. Parker that her husband was ill with consumption.

Correct Answers, Part A _____

Correct Answers, Part B _____

Total Correct Answers _____

from **The Last Leaf**
by O. Henry

Johnsy's eyes were wide open as she looked out the window and counted—counted backward.

"Twelve," she said, and a little later "eleven"; and then "ten," and "nine"; and then "eight" and "seven," almost together.

Sue looked solicitously out of the window. What was there to count? There was only a bare dreary yard to be seen, and the blank side of the brick house twenty feet away. An old, old ivy vine, gnarled and decayed at the roots, climbed halfway up the brick wall. The cold breath of autumn had stricken the leaves from the vine until its skeleton branches clung, almost bare, to the crumbling bricks.

"What is it, dear?" asked Sue.

"Six," said Johnsy, in almost a whisper; "they're falling faster now. Three days ago there were almost a hundred. It made my head ache to count them; but now it's easy. There goes another one; there are only five left now."

"Five what, dear? Tell your Sudie."

"Leaves. On the ivy vine. When the last one falls I must go, too. I've known that for three days. Didn't the doctor tell you?"

"Oh, I never heard of such nonsense," complained Sue, with magnificent scorn. "What have old ivy leaves to do with your getting well? And you used to love that vine so, you naughty girl. Don't be a goosey. Why, the doctor told me this morning that your chances for getting well real soon were—let's see exactly what he said—he said the chances were ten to one! Why, that's almost as good a chance as we have in New York when we ride on the streetcars or walk past a new building. Try to take some broth now, and let Sudie go back to her drawing, so she can sell the editor man with it, and buy port wine for her sick child, and pork chops for her greedy self."

"You needn't get any more wine," said Johnsy, keeping her eyes fixed out the window. "There goes another. No, I don't want any broth. That leaves just four. I want to see the last one fall before it gets dark; then I'll go, too."

"Johnsy, dear," said Sue, bending over her, "will you promise me to keep your eyes closed, and not look out the window until I am done working? I must hand those drawings in by tomorrow and I need the light."

Reading Time _____

Recalling Facts

1. Johnsy is counting
   ❑ a. vines.
   ❑ b. raindrops.
   ❑ c. leaves.

2. This passage takes place during the
   ❑ a. fall.
   ❑ b. spring.
   ❑ c. summer.

3. Sue thinks Johnsy's counting is
   ❑ a. interesting.
   ❑ b. nonsense.
   ❑ c. amusing.

4. Sue works as
   ❑ a. a writer.
   ❑ b. an artist.
   ❑ c. a nurse.

5. Johnsy says she doesn't want any
   ❑ a. broth.
   ❑ b. wine.
   ❑ c. both a and b.

Understanding the Passage

6. Sue finds Johnsy's behavior
   ❑ a. healthy.
   ❑ b. strange.
   ❑ c. typical.

7. Johnsy feels that she is about to
   ❑ a. die.
   ❑ b. get well.
   ❑ c. believe the doctor.

8. According to Sue, the doctor said that Johnsy's chances for recovery were
   ❑ a. very good.
   ❑ b. only fair.
   ❑ c. poor.

9. Sue is anxious to
   ❑ a. join in the counting.
   ❑ b. shop for wine and food.
   ❑ c. get back to her work.

10. Johnsy is anxious to
    ❑ a. eat her supper.
    ❑ b. see the last leaf fall.
    ❑ c. get some sleep.

5 B *from* **White Fang**
by Jack London

Henry sat down on the sled and watched. There was nothing else for him
to do. Bill had already gone from sight; but now and again, appearing and
disappearing amongst the underbrush and the scattered clumps of spruce,
could be seen One Ear. Henry judged his case to be hopeless. The dog was
thoroughly alive to its danger, but it was running on the outer circle while
the wolf-pack was running on the inner and shorter circle. It was vain to
think of One Ear so outdistancing his pursuers as to be able to cut across
their circle in advance of them and to regain the sled.

The different lines were rapidly approaching a point. Somewhere out
there in the snow, screened from his sight by trees and thickets, Henry knew
that the wolf-pack, One Ear, and Bill were coming together. All too quickly,
far more quickly than he had expected, it happened. He heard a shot, then
two shots in rapid succession, and he knew that Bill's ammunition was gone.
Then he heard a great outcry of snarls and yelps. He recognized One Ear's
yell of pain and terror, and he heard a wolf cry that bespoke a stricken
animal. And that was all. The snarls ceased. The yelping died away. Silence
settled down again over the lonely land.

1. **Recognizing Words in Context**

   Find the word *ceased* in the passage.
   One definition below is closest to
   the meaning of that word. One
   definition has the opposite or nearly
   the opposite meaning. The remaining
   definition has a completely different
   meaning. Label each definition C for
   closest, O for *opposite or nearly opposite,*
   or D for *different.*

   _____ a. began

   _____ b. spread

   _____ c. stopped

2. **Keeping Events in Order**

   Number each statement below 1, 2,
   or 3 to show the order in which the
   events took place.

   _____ a. Silence settles over the
   land.

   _____ b. The wolf-pack, One Ear,
   and Bill meet up.

   _____ c. Henry sits down on the
   sled.

3. Making Evaluations

Two of the statements below describe things that actually happen or are stated in the passage. The other statement is an evaluation, or a judgment or opinion, about a character, setting, or event in the passage. Label each statement E for *evaluation* or H for *happens or is stated in the passage.*

_____ a. Henry cares deeply about One Ear's fate.

_____ b. Henry hears an outcry of snarls and yelps.

_____ c. Henry thinks One Ear's case is hopeless.

4. Making Correct Inferences

Two of the statements below are correct inferences, or reasonable guesses. They are based on information in the passage. The other statement is an incorrect, or faulty, inference. Label each statement C for *correct* inference or F for *faulty* inference.

_____ a. Henry and Bill have been traveling together.

_____ b. Bill was trying to save One Ear from the wolves.

_____ c. Henry planned for One Ear to meet up with the wolves.

5. Summarizing

One of the statements below is a summary that tells the most important ideas in the passage. The other two statements contain details from the passage. They do not tell the most important ideas in the passage. Label each statement S for *summary* or D for *details.*

_____ a. One Ear is on the outer circle, and the wolves are on the inner circle.

_____ b. Henry listens as Bill, One Ear, and the wolves meet up and fight.

_____ c. After three shots, Henry knows that Bill's ammunition is gone.

Correct Answers, Part A _____

Correct Answers, Part B _____

Total Correct Answers _____

from **The Ugly Duckling**
by Hans Christian Andersen

The place was as much of a wilderness as the densest wood, and there sat a duck on her nest; she was busy hatching her ducklings, but she was almost tired of it, because sitting is such a tedious business, and she had very few callers. The other ducks thought it more fun to swim about in the moat than to come and have a gossip with her under a wild rhubarb leaf.

At last one eggshell after another began to crack open. "Cheep, cheep!" All the yolks had come to life and were sticking out their heads.

"Quack, quack," said the duck, and all her ducklings came scurrying out as fast as they could, looking about under the green leaves, and their mother let them look as much as they liked, because green is good for the eyes.

"How big the world is!" said all the ducklings, for they felt much more comfortable now than when they were lying in the egg.

"Do you imagine this is the whole of the world?" asked their mother. "It goes far beyond the other side of the garden, right into the Rector's field, but I've never been there yet. I hope you're all here," she went on, and hoisted herself up. "No, I haven't got all of you even now; the biggest egg is still there. I wonder how much longer it will take! I'm getting rather bored with the whole thing." And she squatted down again on the nest.

"Well, how are you getting on?" asked an old duck who came to call on her.

"That last egg is taking an awfully long time," said the brooding duck. "It won't break; but let me show you the others, they're the sweetest ducklings I've ever seen. They are all exactly like their father; the scamp—he never comes to see me!"

"Let me look at the egg that won't break," said the old duck. "You may be sure it's a turkey's egg. I was fooled like that once, and the trouble and bother I had with those youngsters, because they were actually afraid of the water! I simply couldn't get them to go in! I quacked at them and I snapped at them, but it was no use. Let me see the egg—of course it's a turkey's egg. Leave it alone, and teach the other children to swim."

Reading Time _____

Recalling Facts

1. The mother duck finds sitting on her eggs to be
   - ❏ a. fun.
   - ❏ b. easy.
   - ❏ c. boring.

2. Other ducks
   - ❏ a. come to visit the mother duck often.
   - ❏ b. prefer to swim rather than visit the mother duck.
   - ❏ c. offer to sit on the eggs for the mother duck.

3. The mother duck thinks a good color to look at is
   - ❏ a. red.
   - ❏ b. yellow.
   - ❏ c. green.

4. The last unhatched egg is the
   - ❏ a. smallest.
   - ❏ b. biggest.
   - ❏ c. weakest.

5. The old duck thinks that the last egg is a
   - ❏ a. turkey's egg.
   - ❏ b. duck's egg.
   - ❏ c. chicken's egg.

Understanding the Passage

6. The young ducklings are
   - ❏ a. happy to be out of their shells.
   - ❏ b. blind at first.
   - ❏ c. anxious to run away.

7. The young ducklings think that
   - ❏ a. they should go beyond the Rector's field.
   - ❏ b. the whole world consists only of what they can see.
   - ❏ c. the last egg will be the best.

8. The failure of the last egg to crack
   - ❏ a. delights the mother duck.
   - ❏ b. frustrates the mother duck.
   - ❏ c. makes the mother duck furious.

9. The mother duck is unhappy with
   - ❏ a. her ducklings.
   - ❏ b. the ducklings' father.
   - ❏ c. the old duck.

10. The most important skill for a young duckling to learn is
    - ❏ a. sitting on eggs.
    - ❏ b. swimming.
    - ❏ c. hiding from the Rector.

from Ramona, a Story
by Helen Hunt Jackson

Ramona had a cloth-of-gold rose in her hand. The veranda eaves were now shaded with them, hanging down like a thick fringe of golden tassels. It was the rose Felipe loved best. Stooping, she laid it on the bed, near Felipe's head. "He will like to see it when he wakes," she said.

The Señora seized it, and flung it far out in the room. "Take it away! Flowers are poison when one is ill," she said coldly. "Have I never told you that?"

"No, Señora," replied Ramona, meekly; and she glanced at the saucer of musk which the Señora kept on the table close to Felipe's pillow.

"The musk is different," said the Señora, seeing the glance. "Musk is a medicine. It revives."

Ramona knew, but she would have never dared to say, that Felipe hated musk. Many times he had said to her how he hated the odor; but his mother was so fond of it, that it must always be that the veranda and the house would be full of it. Ramona hated it too. At times it made her faint. But neither she nor Felipe would have confessed as much to the Señora. And if they had, she would have thought it all a fancy.

1. **Recognizing Words in Context**

   Find the word *meekly* in the passage. One definition below is closest to the meaning of that word. One definition has the opposite or nearly the opposite meaning. The remaining definition has a completely different meaning. Label each definition C for *closest*, O for *opposite or nearly opposite*, or D for *different*.

   _____ a. oddly

   _____ b. boldly

   _____ c. timidly

2. **Keeping Events in Order**

   Number each statement below 1, 2, or 3 to show the order in which the events took place.

   _____ a. Ramona lays the cloth-of-gold rose near Felipe's head.

   _____ b. The Señora tells Ramona that musk is medicine.

   _____ c. The Señora flings the cloth-of-gold rose.

3. Making Evaluations

Two of the statements below describe things that actually happen or are stated in the passage. The other statement is an evaluation, or a judgment or opinion, about a character, setting, or event in the passage. Label each statement E for *evaluation* or H for *happens or is stated in the passage.*

_____ a. Ramona hates the odor of musk.

_____ b. The Señora treats Ramona cruelly.

_____ c. The Señora says flowers are poison.

4. Making Correct Inferences

Two of the statements below are correct inferences, or reasonable guesses. They are based on information in the passage. The other statement is an incorrect, or faulty, inference. Label each statement C for *correct* inference or F for *faulty* inference.

_____ a. Ramona and the Señora both want Felipe to recover.

_____ b. Ramona loves Felipe more than the Señora does.

_____ c. The Señora is Felipe's mother.

5. Summarizing

One of the statements below is a summary that tells the most important ideas in the passage. The other two statements contain details from the passage. They do not tell the most important ideas in the passage. Label each statement S for *summary* or D for *details.*

_____ a. Ramona and the Señora have different ideas about how to help Felipe.

_____ b. Ramona lays Felipe's favorite kind of rose on the bed near his head.

_____ c. Felipe hates the odor of musk, but his mother is very fond of it.

Correct Answers, Part A _____

Correct Answers, Part B _____

Total Correct Answers _____

from **Strong Hans**

by The Brothers Grimm

There were once a man and a woman who had an only child. They lived quite alone in a solitary valley. It came to pass that the mother once went into the woods to gather branches of fir. She took with her little Hans, who was just two years old. As it was springtime, and the child took pleasure in the many-colored flowers, she went still further onwards with him into the forest. Suddenly two robbers sprang out of the thicket. They seized the mother and child, and carried them far away into the black forest. The poor woman urgently begged the robbers to set her and her child free. But their hearts were made of stone. They would not listen to her prayers and drove her on farther by force. After they had worked their way through bushes and briars for about two miles, they came to a rock where there was a door, at which the robbers knocked and it opened at once. They had to go through a long dark passage. At last they came into a great cavern which was lighted by a fire which burnt on the hearth. On the wall hung swords, sabers, and other deadly weapons which gleamed in the light. In the midst stood a black table at which four other robbers were sitting gambling. The captain sat at the head of it. As soon as he saw the woman he came and spoke to her, and told her to be at ease and have no fear, they would do nothing to hurt her, but she must look after the housekeeping. If she kept everything in order, she should not fare ill with them. Thereupon they gave her something to eat. They showed her a bed where she might sleep with her child.

The woman stayed many years with the robbers, and Hans grew tall and strong. His mother told him stories, and taught him to read an old book of tales about knights which she found in the cave. When Hans was nine years old, he made himself a strong club out of a branch of fir, hid it behind the bed, and then went to his mother and said, "Dear mother, pray tell me who is my father. I must and will know." His mother was silent and would not tell him, that he might not become homesick.

Reading Time _____

Recalling Facts

1. Hans and his parents lived
   - ❑ a. on top of a mountain.
   - ❑ b. alone in a valley.
   - ❑ c. in a small town.

2. Hans and his mother went into the woods to
   - ❑ a. hunt for deer.
   - ❑ b. pick blueberries.
   - ❑ c. gather branches.

3. Hans and his mother are attacked by
   - ❑ a. two robbers.
   - ❑ b. four robbers.
   - ❑ c. six robbers.

4. The captain of the robbers wants Hans's mother to
   - ❑ a. do the housekeeping.
   - ❑ b. chop firewood.
   - ❑ c. leave Hans with them.

5. Hans's mother teaches him to read stories about
   - ❑ a. robbers.
   - ❑ b. heroes.
   - ❑ c. knights.

Understanding the Passage

6. The mother goes further into the forest to
   - ❑ a. please her son.
   - ❑ b. build a hut.
   - ❑ c. visit with neighbors.

7. The robbers who kidnap the mother and her son are
   - ❑ a. quiet and uncertain.
   - ❑ b. interested only in money.
   - ❑ c. threatening and coldhearted.

8. The robbers who kidnap the mother and her son appear to be
   - ❑ a. part of a larger gang.
   - ❑ b. very familiar with the forest.
   - ❑ c. both a and b.

9. The captain wants to
   - ❑ a. ignore his captives.
   - ❑ b. punish his captives.
   - ❑ c. treat his captives fairly.

10. Apparently, Hans does not remember
    - ❑ a. his father.
    - ❑ b. his mother.
    - ❑ c. his age.

from Narrative of the Life of Frederick Douglass
by Frederick Douglass

Mr. Covey soon called out to Hughes for help. Hughes came, and, while Covey held me, attempted to tie my right hand. While he was in the act of doing so, I watched my chance, and gave him a heavy kick close under the ribs. This kick fairly sickened Hughes, so that he left me in the hands of Mr. Covey. This kick had the effect of not only weakening Hughes, but Covey also. When he saw Hughes bending over with pain, his courage quailed. He asked me if I meant to persist in my resistance. I told him I did, come what might; that he had used me like a brute for six months, and that I was determined to be used so no longer. With that, he strove to drag me to a stick that was lying just out of the stable door. He meant to knock me down. But just as he was leaning over to get the stick, I seized him with both hands by his collar, and brought him by a sudden snatch to the ground. By this time, Bill came. Covey called upon him for assistance.

1. **Recognizing Words in Context**

   Find the word *quailed* in the passage. One definition below is closest to the meaning of that word. One definition has the opposite or nearly the opposite meaning. The remaining definition has a completely different meaning. Label each definition C for *closest*, O for *opposite or nearly opposite*, or D for *different*.

   _____ a. failed

   _____ b. grew

   _____ c. followed

2. **Keeping Events in Order**

   Number each statement below 1, 2, or 3 to show the order in which the events took place.

   _____ a. Covey calls to Bill for help.

   _____ b. The narrator kicks Hughes under the ribs.

   _____ c. The narrator knocks Covey to the ground.

3. Making Evaluations

Two of the statements below describe things that actually happen or are stated in the passage. The other statement is an evaluation, or a judgment or opinion, about a character, setting, or event in the passage. Label each statement E for *evaluation* or H for *happens or is stated in the passage.*

_____ a. The narrator's kick weakens both Hughes and Covey.

_____ b. Covey calls out to Hughes for assistance.

_____ c. The narrator acts bravely and with determination.

4. Making Correct Inferences

Two of the statements below are correct inferences, or reasonable guesses. They are based on information in the passage. The other statement is an incorrect, or faulty, inference. Label each statement C for *correct* inference or F for *faulty* inference.

_____ a. Covey does not feel confident that he can overpower the narrator.

_____ b. The narrator is being forced to work for Covey.

_____ c. The narrator is trying to kill Covey.

5. Summarizing

One of the statements below is a summary that tells the most important ideas in the passage. The other two statements contain details from the passage. They do not tell the most important ideas in the passage. Label each statement S for *summary* or D for *details.*

_____ a. Covey drags the narrator over to a stick outside the stable door.

_____ b. The narrator kicks Hughes under the ribs, and Hughes bends over in pain.

_____ c. The narrator rebels against Covey, and Covey needs help to fight him off.

Correct Answers, Part A _____

Correct Answers, Part B _____

Total Correct Answers _____

Smith locked up his room. He then went home for the first time in two months, telephoned for a stateroom on the Western Limited, and sent for Kerns, who arrived in an electric cab.

"I'm going to Illinois," said Smith, "tonight."

"The nation must know of this," said Kerns. "Let me wire ahead for fireworks."

"There'll be fireworks," observed Smith—"fireworks to burn. I'm going to get married to a working girl."

"Oh, piffle!" said Kerns faintly. "Let's go and sit on the third rail and talk it over."

"Not with *you,* idiot. Did you ever hear of Stanley Stevens, who tried to corner wheat? I think it's his daughter I'm going to marry. I'm going to Chicago to find out. Good heavens, Kerns! It's the most pitiful case, whoever she is! It's a case to stir the manhood of any man. I tell you it's got to be righted. I am thoroughly stirred up, and I won't stand any nonsense from you."

Kerns looked at him. "Smith," he pleaded in grave tones; "Smithy! For the sake of decency and of common sense—"

"Exactly," nodded Smith, picking up his hat and gloves; "for the sake of decency and of common sense. Good-bye Tommy. And—ah!"—pointing to a parcel of papers on the desk—"just have an architect look over these sketches with a view to estimating the—ah—cost of construction. And find some good landscape gardener to figure up what it will cost to remove a big ailanthus tree from New York to the Berkshires. You can tell him I'll sue him if he injures the tree. But I don't care what it costs to move it."

"Smith!" faltered Kerns, "you're as mad as Hamlet!"

"It's one of my goals to be madder," retorted Smith, going out and running nimbly downstairs.

"Help!" observed Kerns feebly as the front door slammed. And, as nobody responded, he sat down in the bachelor quarters of J. Abingdon Smith, a prey to melancholy amazement.

When Smith had been gone a week Kerns wrote him. When he had been gone two weeks he telegraphed him. When the third week ended he telephoned him. And when the month was up he prepared to leave for darkest Chicago. In fact he was actually leaving his house, suitcase in hand, when Smith drove up in a hansom and gleefully waved his hand.

Reading Time _____

Recalling Facts

1. Smith tells Kerns he is planning to travel to
   - ❏ a. Indiana.
   - ❏ b. Illinois.
   - ❏ c. Iowa.

2. Smith says he is going to marry a
   - ❏ a. working girl.
   - ❏ b. rich girl.
   - ❏ c. farm girl.

3. Stanley Stevens tried to corner the market in
   - ❏ a. gold.
   - ❏ b. construction materials.
   - ❏ c. wheat.

4. Smith wants someone to move a
   - ❏ a. stateroom.
   - ❏ b. particular tree.
   - ❏ c. group of animals.

5. After Smith has been gone for a month, Kerns
   - ❏ a. writes him.
   - ❏ b. telegraphs him.
   - ❏ c. prepares to leave for Chicago.

Understanding the Passage

6. Smith appears to
   - ❏ a. have enough money to do what he wishes.
   - ❏ b. be afraid to travel too far from home.
   - ❏ c. be in need of an expert lawyer.

7. Smith is
   - ❏ a. not willing to travel on a train.
   - ❏ b. not very familiar with his future bride's family.
   - ❏ c. a man lacking in decency and common sense.

8. Kerns appears to
   - ❏ a. be afraid of Smith.
   - ❏ b. dislike Smith.
   - ❏ c. know Smith quite well.

9. Smith feels very strongly about
   - ❏ a. saving a lot of money.
   - ❏ b. staying in New York.
   - ❏ c. moving the ailanthus tree.

10. Smith's marriage plans
    - ❏ a. delight Kerns.
    - ❏ b. surprise Kerns.
    - ❏ c. are delayed by Kerns.

| 8 | B | | *from* **The Moonstone** |

by Wilkie Collins

About half-past seven in the morning I woke, and opened my window on a fine sunshiny day. The clock had struck eight, and I was just going out to chain up the dogs again, when I heard a sudden whisking of petticoats on the stairs behind me.

I quickly turned around. There was Penelope flying down after me like mad. "Father!" she screamed, "come up stairs, for God's sake! *The Diamond is gone!*"

"Are you out of your mind?" I asked her.

"Gone!" says Penelope. "Gone, nobody knows how! Come up and see for yourself."

She dragged me after her into her young lady's sitting room, which opened into her bedroom. There, on the threshold of her bedroom door, stood Miss Rachel. The poor girl was almost as white in the face as the white dressing gown that clothed her. There also stood the two doors of the Indian cabinet, wide open. One of the drawers inside was pulled out as far as it would go.

"Look!" says Penelope. "I myself saw Miss Rachel put the Diamond into that drawer last night."

I went to the cabinet. The drawer was empty.

1. **Recognizing Words in Context**

   Find the word *threshold* in the passage. One definition below is closest to the meaning of that word. One definition has the opposite or nearly the opposite meaning. The remaining definition has a completely different meaning. Label each definition C for *closest*, O for *opposite or nearly opposite*, or D for *different*.

   _____ a. last part

   _____ b. entrance

   _____ c. room

2. **Keeping Events in Order**

   Number each statement below 1, 2, or 3 to show the order in which the events took place.

   _____ a. The narrator hears the whisking of Penelope's petticoats.

   _____ b. Penelope drags the narrator to Miss Rachel's bedroom.

   _____ c. Penelope sees Miss Rachel put the Diamond into the drawer.

3. Making Evaluations

Two of the statements below describe things that actually happen or are stated in the passage. The other statement is an evaluation, or a judgment or opinion, about a character, setting, or event in the passage. Label each statement E for *evaluation* or H for *happens or is stated in the passage.*

_____ a. The narrator asks if Penelope is out of her mind.

_____ b. Penelope is overly dramatic about the Diamond.

_____ c. Miss Rachel is white in the face.

4. Making Correct Inferences

Two of the statements below are correct inferences, or reasonable guesses. They are based on information in the passage. The other statement is an incorrect, or faulty, inference. Label each statement C for *correct* inference or F for *faulty* inference.

_____ a. Miss Rachel is not allowed to handle the Diamond.

_____ b. Miss Rachel works in the home of Penelope and the narrator.

_____ c. Miss Rachel is afraid she will be blamed for the missing Diamond.

5. Summarizing

One of the statements below is a summary that tells the most important ideas in the passage. The other two statements contain details from the passage. They do not tell the most important ideas in the passage. Label each statement S for *summary* or D for *details.*

_____ a. The narrator opens the window on a fine, sunshiny day.

_____ b. Penelope tells the narrator that the Diamond has mysteriously vanished.

_____ c. The doors of Miss Rachel's Indian cabinet are wide open.

Correct Answers, Part A _____

Correct Answers, Part B _____

Total Correct Answers _____

9 | A | *from* **Life in the Iron Mills**
by Rebecca Harding Davis

It was market day. The narrow window of the jail looked down directly on the carts and wagons drawn up in a long line, where they had unloaded. Hugh could see, too, and hear distinctly the clink of money as it changed hands, and busy crowd shoving, pushing one another, and swearing at the stalls. Somehow, the sound, more than anything else had done, woke him up—made the whole real to him. He was done with the world and the business of it. He looked out, pressing his face close to the rusty bars. How they crowded and pushed! And he—he should never walk that pavement again! There came Neff Sanders with a basket on his arm. Sure enough, Neff was married the other week. He whistled, hoping he would look up; but he did not. He wondered if Neff remembered he was there—if any of the boys thought of him up there, and thought that he never was to go down that old cinder road again. Never again! He had not quite understood it before; but now he did. Not for days or years, but never!— that was it.

How clear the light fell on that stall in front of the market! How like a picture it was, the dark green heaps of corn, and the crimson beets, and golden melons! There was another with game: how the light flickered on that pheasant's breast, with the purplish blood dripping over the brown feathers! He could see the red shining of the drops, it was so near. In one minute he could be down there. It was just a step. So easy, as it seemed, so natural to go! Yet it could never be—not in all the thousands of years to come—that he should put his foot on that street again! He tried to put the thought away, but it would come back. He, what had he done to bear this?

Then came the sudden picture of what might have been, and now. He knew what it was to be in the penitentiary—how it went with men there. He knew how in these long years he should slowly die, but not until soul and body had become corrupt and rotten—how, when he came out, if he lived to come, even the lowest mill hands would jeer him—how his hands would be weak, and his brain senseless and stupid.

Reading Time _____

Recalling Facts

1. Hugh's window looks out over
   - ❏ a. a school yard.
   - ❏ b. the marketplace.
   - ❏ c. the warden's home.

2. Neff Sanders has recently been
   - ❏ a. arrested.
   - ❏ b. married.
   - ❏ c. in to visit Hugh.

3. Neff comes to market carrying a
   - ❏ a. pheasant.
   - ❏ b. barrel of corn.
   - ❏ c. basket.

4. To get Neff's attention, Hugh
   - ❏ a. bangs on the bars.
   - ❏ b. whistles.
   - ❏ c. calls out.

5. Hugh believes that in prison his hands will
   - ❏ a. be broken.
   - ❏ b. develop calluses.
   - ❏ c. become weak.

Understanding the Passage

6. Apparently, Hugh has been sentenced to
   - ❏ a. a few months in jail.
   - ❏ b. three years in jail.
   - ❏ c. many years in jail.

7. The sounds of the marketplace makes Hugh realize
   - ❏ a. how much people miss him.
   - ❏ b. how sad his situation really is.
   - ❏ c. that prison is not such a bad place.

8. Hugh has probably not been
   - ❏ a. visited by Neff and the boys.
   - ❏ b. given any food.
   - ❏ c. able to write any letters.

9. Hugh longs to
   - ❏ a. talk to his family.
   - ❏ b. walk through the streets.
   - ❏ c. have a decent meal.

10. The penitentiary is a
    - ❏ a. depressing place.
    - ❏ b. temporary prison.
    - ❏ c. place for execution.

from **Buried Alive**
by Arnold Bennett

Priam Farll's eyes fell on the coffin of Henry Leek with its white cross. And there was the end of Priam Farll's self-control. A pang seized him, and an issuing sob nearly ripped him in two. It was a loud sob, undisguised and unashamed. Other sobs succeeded it. Priam Farll was in torture. The organist vaulted over his seat, shocked by the outrage. "You really mustn't make that noise," whispered the organist.

Priam Farll shook him off.

The organist was apparently at a loss what to do.

"Who is it?" whispered one of the young men.

"Don't know him from Adam!" said the organist with conviction, and then to Priam Farll: "Who are you? You've no right to be here. Who gave you permission to come up here?" The rending sobs continued to issue from the full-bodied man of fifty.

"It's perfectly absurd!" whispered the youngster who had whispered before.

"Here! They're waiting for you!" whispered the other young man excitedly to the organist.

"By—!" whispered the alarmed organist, not stopping to say by what, but leaping like an acrobat back to his seat. His fingers and boots were at work instantly, and as he played he turned his head and whispered: "Better fetch someone to give us a hand."

1. **Recognizing Words in Context**

   Find the word *conviction* in the passage. One definition below is closest to the meaning of that word. One definition has the opposite or nearly the opposite meaning. The remaining definition has a completely different meaning. Label the definitions C for *closest*, O for *opposite or nearly opposite*, and D for *different*.

   _____ a. uncertainty

   _____ b. innocence

   _____ c. sureness

2. **Keeping Events in Order**

   Number each statement below 1, 2, or 3 to show the order in which the events took place.

   _____ a. The organist tells Priam Farll not to make noise.

   _____ b. Priam Farll sees the coffin of Henry Leek.

   _____ c. The organist leaps back to his seat.

3. Making Evaluations

Two of the statements below describe things that actually happen or are stated in the passage. The other statement is an evaluation, or a judgment or opinion, about a character, setting, or event in the passage. Label each statement E for *evaluation* or H for *happens or is stated in the passage*.

_____ a. The young men treat Priam Farll very coldly.

_____ b. The organist does not know Priam Farll.

_____ c. Priam Farll loses his self-control.

4. Making Correct Inferences

Two of the statements below are correct inferences, or reasonable guesses. They are based on information in the passage. The other statement is an incorrect, or faulty, inference. Label each statement C for *correct* inference or F for *faulty* inference.

_____ a. The organist was a close friend of Henry Leek.

_____ b. The story takes place during a funeral service.

_____ c. Priam Farll is upset that Henry Leek is dead.

5. Summarizing

One of the statements below is a summary that tells the most important ideas in the passage. The other two statements contain details from the passage. They do not tell the most important ideas in the passage. Label each statement S for *summary* or D for *details*.

_____ a. Priam Farll sobs when he sees the coffin, and the organist tries to quiet him.

_____ b. The organist vaults over his seat, shocked by the noise Priam Farll is making.

_____ c. Two young men whisper to the organist as he speaks to Priam Farll.

Correct Answers, Part A _____

Correct Answers, Part B _____

Total Correct Answers _____

10 | A | *from* **The Club of Queer Trades**
by G. K. Chesterton

"Which man?" I cried, and then my eye caught the figure at which Basil Grant's bull's eyes were glaring.

"What has he done?" I asked.

"I am not sure of the details," said Grant, "but his sin is a desire to intrigue to the disadvantage of others. Probably he has adopted some act or other to effect his plan."

"What plan?" I asked. "If you know all about him why don't you tell me why he is the wickedest man in England? What is his name?"

Basil Grant stared at me for some moments.

"I think you've made a mistake in my meaning," he said. "I don't know his name. I never saw him before in my life."

"Never saw him before!" I cried, with a kind of anger. "Then what in Heaven's name do you mean by saying that he is the wickedest man in England?"

"I meant what I said," said Basil Grant, calmly. "The moment I saw that man I saw all these people stricken with a sudden innocence. I saw that while all ordinary poor men in these streets were being themselves, he was not being himself. I saw that all the men in these slums—cadgers, pick-pockets, hooligans—are all, in the deepest sense, trying to be good. And I saw that that man was trying to be evil."

"But if you never saw him before—" I began.

"In God's name, look at his face," cried out Basil, in a voice that startled the driver. "Look at the eyebrows. They mean that infernal pride which made Satan so proud that he sneered even at heaven when he was one of the first angels in it. Look at his mustaches! They are so grown as to insult humanity. In the name of the sacred heavens, look at his hair. In the name of God and the stars, look at his hat."

I stirred uncomfortably.

"But after all," I said, "this is very fanciful—perfectly absurd. Look at the mere facts. You have never seen the man before you—"

"Oh, the mere facts," he cried out, in a kind of despair. "The mere facts! Do you really admit—are you still so sunk in superstitions, so clinging to dim and prehistoric altars, that you believe in facts? Do you not trust an immediate impression?"

"Well, an immediate impression may be," I said, "a little less practical than facts."

Reading Time _____

Recalling Facts

1. Basil Grant does not know the man's
   - ❏ a. name.
   - ❏ b. plan.
   - ❏ c. both a and b.

2. Basil calls the man the wickedest man in
   - ❏ a. New England.
   - ❏ b. England.
   - ❏ c. Ireland.

3. Basil says that most men in the slums are trying to be
   - ❏ a. good.
   - ❏ b. happy.
   - ❏ c. evil.

4. One of the man's features that catches Basil's eye is his
   - ❏ a. nose.
   - ❏ b. eyebrows.
   - ❏ c. forehead.

5. The narrator is most interested in
   - ❏ a. people's looks.
   - ❏ b. first impressions.
   - ❏ c. the facts.

Understanding the Passage

6. Basil appears to be
   - ❏ a. uncertain.
   - ❏ b. confident.
   - ❏ c. cautious.

7. Basil obviously trusts his
   - ❏ a. research.
   - ❏ b. instincts.
   - ❏ c. education.

8. The man's evil nature is
   - ❏ a. not apparent to the narrator.
   - ❏ b. noticed by everyone except the narrator.
   - ❏ c. overlooked by Basil.

9. The narrator believes facts are
   - ❏ a. often misleading.
   - ❏ b. usually used to mask the truth.
   - ❏ c. more practical than impressions.

10. Basil's comments about the man are
   - ❏ a. confusing.
   - ❏ b. expected.
   - ❏ c. depressing.

from The Octopus
by Frank Norris

It was about half-past three. "If we have passed Fresno," he said to himself, "I'd better wake the little girl pretty soon. She'll need about an hour to dress. Better find out for sure."

He drew on his trousers and shoes, got into his coat, and stepped out into the aisle. In the seat that had been occupied by the porter, the Pullman conductor, his cash box and car schedules before him, was checking up his berths, a blue pencil behind his ear.

"What's the next stop, captain?" inquired Annixter, coming up. "Have we reached Fresno yet?"

"Just passed it," the other responded, looking at Annixter over his spectacles.

"What's the next stop?"

"Goshen. We will be there in about forty-five minutes."

"Fair black night, isn't it?"

"Black as a pocket. Let's see, you're the party in upper and lower 9."

Annixter caught at the back of the nearest seat just in time to prevent a fall, and the conductor's cash box was shunted off the surface of the plush seat and came clanking to the floor. The lights overhead vibrated with blinding speed in the long, sliding jar that ran through the train from end to end, and the momentum of its speed suddenly decreasing, all but pitched the conductor from his seat.

1. **Recognizing Words in Context**

   Find the word *decreasing* in the passage. One definition below is closest to the meaning of that word. One definition has the opposite or nearly the opposite meaning. The remaining definition has a completely different meaning. Label each definition C for *closest*, O for *opposite or nearly opposite*, or D for *different*.

   _____ a. shaking

   _____ b. slowing

   _____ c. quickening

2. **Keeping Events in Order**

   Number each statement below 1, 2, or 3 to show the order in which the events took place.

   _____ a. Annixter puts on his trousers, shoes, and coat.

   _____ b. Annixter asks the conductor if the train has passed Fresno.

   _____ c. Annixter grabs for the back of a seat so he doesn't fall.

3. Making Evaluations

Two of the statements below describe things that actually happen or are stated in the passage. The other statement is an evaluation, or a judgment or opinion, about a character, setting, or event in the passage. Label each statement E for *evaluation* or H for *happens or is stated in the passage.*

_____ a. Annixter has a conversation with the conductor.

_____ b. Annixter is thoughtful about the little girl's needs.

_____ c. The conductor is almost pitched from his seat.

4. Making Correct Inferences

Two of the statements below are correct inferences, or reasonable guesses. They are based on information in the passage. The other statement is an incorrect, or faulty, inference. Label the statements C for *correct* inference or F for *faulty* inference.

_____ a. Annixter is traveling with and taking care of a little girl.

_____ b. Annixter does not expect the train's change in speed.

_____ c. Annixter was planning to get off the train at Fresno.

5. Summarizing

One of the statements below is a summary that tells the most important ideas in the passage. The other two statements contain details from the passage. They do not tell the most important ideas in the passage. Label each statements S for *summary* or D for *details.*

_____ a. Annixter believes that the little girl will need about an hour to get dressed.

_____ b. Annixter asks about the train's progress, and suddenly the train slows down.

_____ c. Annixter remarks that the night is fair and black, and the conductor agrees.

Correct Answers, Part A _____

Correct Answers, Part B _____

Total Correct Answers _____

11 A *from* **The Return of the Native**
by Thomas Hardy

When Clym Yeobright was not with Eustacia he was sitting slavishly over his books; when he was not reading he was meeting her. These meetings were carried on with the greatest secrecy.

One afternoon his mother came home from a morning visit to Thomasin. He could see from a disturbance in the lines of her face that something had happened.

"I have been told an incomprehensible thing," she said mournfully. "The captain has let out at the Woman that you and Eustacia Vye are engaged to be married."

"We are," said Clym. "But it may not be for a very long time."

"I should hardly think it *would* be for a very long time! You will take her to Paris, I assume?" She spoke with weary hopelessness.

"I am not going back to Paris."

"What will you do with a wife, then?"

"Keep a school in Budmouth, as I have told you."

"That's foolish! The place is overrun with schoolmasters. You have no special qualifications. What chance is there for you?"

"There is no chance of getting rich. But with my system of education, which is as new as it is true, I shall do a great deal of good to my fellow creatures."

"Dreams, dreams! If there was a system left to be invented they would have found it out at the universities long before this time."

"Never, mother. They cannot find it out, because their teachers don't come in contact with the class which demands such a system—that is, those who have had no preliminary training. My plan is one for instilling high knowledge into empty minds."

"I might have believed you if you had kept yourself free from entanglements; but this woman—if she had been a good girl it would have been bad enough; but being such a—"

"She is a good girl."

"So you think. A Corfu bandmaster's daughter! What has her life been? Her surname even is not her true one."

"She is Captain Vye's granddaughter, and her father merely took her mother's name. And she is a lady by instinct."

"They call him 'captain,' but anybody is captain."

"He was in the Royal Navy!"

"No doubt he has been to sea in some tub or other. Why doesn't he look after her? No lady would rove about the heath at all hours of the day and night as she does."

Reading Time _____

Recalling Facts

1. Clym is engaged to marry
   - ❏ a. Thomasin.
   - ❏ b. Miss Budmouth.
   - ❏ c. Eustacia.

2. Clym admits he has no chance of
   - ❏ a. meeting Captain Vye.
   - ❏ b. going to Paris.
   - ❏ c. getting rich.

3. Eustacia is the daughter of a
   - ❏ a. bandmaster.
   - ❏ b. schoolmaster.
   - ❏ c. circus master.

4. Eustacia is Captain Vye's
   - ❏ a. daughter.
   - ❏ b. granddaughter.
   - ❏ c. sister.

5. Captain Vye spent some time in
   - ❏ a. prison.
   - ❏ b. the Royal Navy.
   - ❏ c. America.

Understanding the Passage

6. Clym's mother does not
   - ❏ a. approve of her son's engagement.
   - ❏ b. know what Thomasin looks like.
   - ❏ c. believe in education.

7. Clym believes Eustacia is
   - ❏ a. a troublemaker.
   - ❏ b. a fine woman.
   - ❏ c. terribly ignorant.

8. Clym has
   - ❏ a. special qualifications to become a teacher.
   - ❏ b. great faith in his system of education.
   - ❏ c. never completed high school.

9. Clym's mother does not think very highly of
   - ❏ a. Eustacia.
   - ❏ b. Captain Vye.
   - ❏ c. both a and b.

10. Clym's mother could best be described as
   - ❏ a. highly critical.
   - ❏ b. generous.
   - ❏ c. easily confused.

from **The Land of Oz**

by L. Frank Baum

Tip was bound so tightly by the cord that he could not turn his head to look at his companions. So he said to the Saw-Horse: "Paddle with your legs toward the shore." The horse obeyed. Although their progress was slow they finally reached the opposite river bank at a place where it was low enough to enable the creature to scramble upon dry land.

Tip managed to get his knife out of his pocket and cut the cords that bound the riders to one another and to the wooden horse. He heard the Scarecrow King fall to the ground with a mushy sound. Then Tip quickly dismounted and looked at his friend Jack.

The wooden body, with its gorgeous clothing, still sat upright upon the horse's back; but the pumpkin head was gone. Only the sharpened stick that served for a neck was visible. As for the Scarecrow King, the straw in his body had shaken down the jolting and packed itself into his legs and the lower part of his body—which appeared very plump and round while his upper half seemed like an empty sack. Upon his head the Scarecrow King still wore the heavy crown. It had been sewed on to prevent his losing it.

1. **Recognizing Words in Context**

   Find the word *bound* in the passage. One definition below is closest to the meaning of that word. One definition has the opposite or nearly the opposite meaning. The remaining definition has a completely different meaning. Label each definition C for *closest,* O for *opposite or nearly opposite,* or D for *different.*

   _____ a. tied

   _____ b. hurt

   _____ c. freed

2. **Keeping Events in Order**

   Number each statement below 1, 2, or 3 to show the order in which the events took place.

   _____ a. Tip and his companions reach the opposite river bank.

   _____ b. Tip tells the Saw-Horse to paddle with its legs.

   _____ c. Tip cuts the cords that tie the riders together.

3. Making Evaluations

Two of the statements below describe things that actually happen or are stated in the passage. The other statement is an evaluation, or a judgment or opinion, about a character, setting, or event in the passage. Label each statement E for *evaluation* or H for *happens or is stated in the passage.*

_____ a. Tip wants to take good care of his traveling companions.

_____ b. The lower part of the Scarecrow King's body appears plump.

_____ c. Tip is bound so tightly that he cannot turn his head.

4. Making Correct Inferences

Two of the statements below are correct inferences, or reasonable guesses. They are based on information in the passage. The other statement is an incorrect, or faulty, inference. Label the statements C for *correct* inference or F for *faulty* inference.

_____ a. The Scarecrow King makes a mushy sound because he is wet.

_____ b. It takes very little time for the group to cross the river.

_____ c. Jack and the Scarecrow King are not humans.

5. Summarizing

One of the statements below is a summary that tells the most important ideas in the passage. The other two statements contain details from the passage. They do not tell the most important ideas in the passage. Label each statements S for *summary* or D for *details.*

_____ a. Tip cuts the cords that hold the members of the group together.

_____ b. The ground is finally low enough for the Saw-Horse to scramble up.

_____ c. The group makes a slow and difficult trip across the river.

Correct Answers, Part A _____

Correct Answers, Part B _____

Total Correct Answers _____

56

12   A   *from* A Journey to the Centre of the Earth

by Jules Verne

I thanked my uncle by clasping my hands. My heart was too full to speak.

"Yes," said he, "one more mouthful of water, the very last—do you hear, my boy?—the very last! I have taken care of it at the bottom of my bottle as the apple of my eye. Twenty times, a hundred times, I have resisted the desire to drink it. But—no—no, Harry, I have saved it for you."

"My dear uncle," I exclaimed, and the big tears rolled down my hot cheeks.

"Yes, my poor boy. I knew that when you reached this place, this crossroad in the earth, you would fall down half dead. I saved my last drop of water in order to restore you."

"Thanks," I cried; "thanks from my heart." I had recovered some of my strength. "Well," I said, "there can be no doubt now as to what we have to do. Our journey is at an end. Let us return."

While I spoke thus, my uncle avoided my face: he held down his head; his eyes were turned in every direction but the right one.

"Yes," I continued, getting excited by my own words, "we must go back to Sneffels. May Heaven give us strength to enable us once more to revisit the light of day. Would that we now stood on the summit of that crater."

"Go back," said my uncle, speaking to himself—"and must it be so?"

"Go back—yes, and without losing a single moment," I cried. For some moments there was silence under that dark and gloomy vault.

"So, my dear Harry," said my uncle the Professor, in a very singular tone of voice, "those few drops of water have not sufficed to restore your courage."

"Courage!" I cried.

"I see that you are quite as downcast as before, and still give way to despair."

What, then, was the man made of, and what other projects were entering his fertile brain?

"You are not discouraged, sir?"

"What! Give up just as we are on the verge of success?" he cried. "Never, never shall it be said that Professor Hardwigg retreated."

"Then we must make up our minds to perish," I cried, with a helpless sigh.

"No, Harry, my boy; certainly not. Go, leave me; I am very far from desiring your death. Take Hans with you. *I will go on alone.*"

Reading Time _____

Recalling Facts

1. The uncle gives Harry
   - ❏ a. a bandage.
   - ❏ b. a piece of an apple.
   - ❏ c. the last drops of water.

2. Harry wants to
   - ❏ a. return to Sneffels.
   - ❏ b. stay just where he is.
   - ❏ c. move on.

3. Harry wishes that he was
   - ❏ a. on the summit of the crater.
   - ❏ b. in the center of the earth.
   - ❏ c. dead.

4. The uncle decides to
   - ❏ a. turn back.
   - ❏ b. make camp.
   - ❏ c. go on alone.

5. The uncle does not want
   - ❏ a. to continue the journey.
   - ❏ b. his nephew to die.
   - ❏ c. the journey to be a success.

Understanding the Passage

6. The uncle
   - ❏ a. wants to drink the water.
   - ❏ b. feels responsible for Harry.
   - ❏ c. both a and b.

7. The uncle had expected
   - ❏ a. Harry to need the water.
   - ❏ b. a smooth voyage.
   - ❏ c. Harry to outlast him.

8. The uncle and Harry
   - ❏ a. share the same enthusiasm.
   - ❏ b. have a disagreement.
   - ❏ c. don't like each other.

9. Harry wants to return
   - ❏ a. after resting a while.
   - ❏ b. only after reaching their goal.
   - ❏ c. immediately.

10. Harry is sure that following his uncle will mean
    - ❏ a. death.
    - ❏ b. success.
    - ❏ c. fame.

12 B | *from* **Peter and Wendy**
by James M. Barrie

The pirates disappeared among the trees, and in a moment their captain and Smee were alone. Hook heaved a heavy sigh, and I know not why it was; perhaps it was because of the soft beauty of the evening, but there came over him a desire to confide to his faithful bo'son his life story. He spoke long and earnestly, but what it was all about, Smee, who was rather stupid, did not know in the least.

Anon he caught the word Peter.

"Most of all," Hook was saying passionately, "I want their captain, Peter Pan. 'Twas he cut off my arm." He brandished the hook threateningly. "I've waited long to shake his hand with this. Oh, I'll tear him!"

"And yet," said Smee, "I have often heard you say that hook was worth a score of hands, for combing the hair and other homely uses."

"Ay," the captain answered, "if I was a mother I would pray to have my children born with this instead of that," and he cast a look of pride upon his iron hand and one of scorn upon the other. Then again he frowned.

---

1. **Recognizing Words in Context**

   Find the word *confide* in the passage. One definition below is closest to the meaning of that word. One definition has the opposite or nearly the opposite meaning. The remaining definition has a completely different meaning. Label each definition C for *closest,* O for *opposite or nearly opposite,* or D for *different.*

   _____ a. tell

   _____ b. hide

   _____ c. sing

2. **Keeping Events in Order**

   Number each statement below 1, 2, or 3 to show the order in which the events took place.

   _____ a. Hook tells Smee his life story.

   _____ b. Hook looks at his remaining hand with scorn.

   _____ c. The pirates disappear among the trees.

3. Making Evaluations

Two of the statements below describe things that actually happen or are stated in the passage. The other statement is an evaluation, or a judgment or opinion, about a character, setting, or event in the passage. Label each statement E for *evaluation* or H for *happens or is stated in the passage.*

_____ a. Smee does not understand most of Hook's life story.

_____ b. Hook brandishes his hook in a threatening way.

_____ c. Hook's pride about his iron hand is rather strange.

4. Making Correct Inferences

Two of the statements below are correct inferences, or reasonable guesses. They are based on information in the passage. The other statement is an incorrect, or faulty, inference. Label the statements C for *correct* inference or F for *faulty* inference.

_____ a. Hook does not trust Smee to be loyal to him.

_____ b. Hook does not usually confide in others so freely.

_____ c. Hook would like to take revenge on Peter Pan.

5. Summarizing

One of the statements below is a summary that tells the most important ideas in the passage. The other two statements contain details from the passage. They do not tell the most important ideas in the passage. Label each statements S for *summary* or D for *details.*

_____ a. Smee does not know what Hook's life story is all about.

_____ b. Hook looks at his hook with pride and at his hand with scorn.

_____ c. Hook tells his life story to Smee and says he wants to attack Peter.

Correct Answers, Part A _____

Correct Answers, Part B _____

Total Correct Answers _____

13 A   *from* **Les Miserables**
by Victor Hugo

Cravatte's rebels desolated the country and the army was in vain placed on his track. In the midst of all this terror the Bishop arrived on his visitation, and the Mayor came to him and urged him to turn back. Cravatte held the mountain as far as Arche and beyond, and there was danger, even with an escort. It would be uselessly exposing three or four unhappy soldiers.

"For that reason," said the Bishop, "I will go without escort."

"Can you mean it, Monseigneur?" the Mayor exclaimed.

"I mean it so fully that I absolutely refuse the soldiers and intend to start within an hour."

"Monseigneur, you will not do that!"

"There is in the mountain," the Bishop continued, "a humble little parish, which I have not visited for three years. They are good friends of mine, and quiet and honest shepherds. They are the owners of one goat out of every thirty they guard; they make very pretty woolen robes of different colors, and they play mountain airs on small six-holed flutes. They want to hear about heaven every now and then, and what would they think of a bishop who was afraid? What would they say if I did not go?"

"But Monseigneur, the rebels."

"Ah," said the Bishop, "you are right; I may meet them. They too must want to hear about heaven."

"But this band is a flock of wolves."

"Monsieur Mayor, it may be that this is precisely the flock of which Christ has made me the shepherd. Who knows the ways of God?"

"Monseigneur, they will plunder you."

"I haven't anything for them to take."

"They will kill you."

"A poor old priest who passes by, muttering his prayers? Nonsense, what good would it do them to kill me?"

"Oh, good gracious, if you were to meet them!"

"I would ask them for alms for my poor."

"Monseigneur, do not go. You will be exposing your life."

"My good sir," said the Bishop, "is that all? I am not in this world to save my life, but to save souls."

There was no help for it; he set out accompanied only by a lad, who offered to act as his guide. His stubbornness created a stir in the country and caused considerable alarm. He crossed the mountain on a mule, met nobody, and reached his friends, the goatherds, safely.

Reading Time _____

Recalling Facts

1. Cravatte is the leader of the
   - ❏ a. church.
   - ❏ b. army.
   - ❏ c. rebels.

2. The Bishop refuses
   - ❏ a. soldiers as an escort.
   - ❏ b. to visit the shepherds.
   - ❏ c. to travel alone.

3. The shepherds play music on
   - ❏ a. stringed instruments.
   - ❏ b. flutes.
   - ❏ c. horns.

4. The Mayor compares the rebels to a
   - ❏ a. band of thieves.
   - ❏ b. flock of wolves.
   - ❏ c. group of misguided pilgrims.

5. The Bishop's guide is
   - ❏ a. an old man.
   - ❏ b. a young lad.
   - ❏ c. a rebel leader.

Understanding the Passage

6. The Mayor is concerned about the Bishop's
   - ❏ a. sanity.
   - ❏ b. safety.
   - ❏ c. religious convictions.

7. The Bishop appears to be
   - ❏ a. very religious.
   - ❏ b. quite fearful.
   - ❏ c. disappointed with the Mayor.

8. The shepherds
   - ❏ a. work for other people.
   - ❏ b. lack any religious faith.
   - ❏ c. are reserved and independent.

9. The Bishop believes that the rebels will
   - ❏ a. kill him.
   - ❏ b. show little interest in him.
   - ❏ c. join the shepherds in the field.

10. The Bishop is very clear about
    - ❏ a. how to find the rebels.
    - ❏ b. his mission in life.
    - ❏ c. both a and b.

13　B　*from* Nevada: a Romance of the West

by Zane Grey

It was still daylight, however, when Nevada went out, to walk leisurely down the road into town. He came at length to the narrow block where there were a few horses and vehicles along the hitching rails, and people passing to and fro. There were several stores and shops, a saloon, and a restaurant, that appeared precisely as they had always been. A Chinaman, standing in a doorway, stared keenly at Nevada. His black eyes showed recognition. Then Nevada arrived at a corner store, where he entered. The place had the smell of general merchandise, groceries, and tobacco combined. To Jones's credit, he had never sold liquor. There was a boy clerk waiting on a woman customer, and Jones, a long lanky Westerner, who had seen range days himself.

"Howdy, Mr. Jones!" said Nevada, stepping forward.

"Howdy yourself, stranger!" replied the storekeeper. "You got the best of me."

"Wal, it's a little dark in heah or your eyes are failin'," returned Nevada, with a grin. Whereupon the other took a stride and bent over to peer into Nevada's face.

"I'm a son of a gun," he declared. "Jim Lacy! Back in Lineville! I've seen fellers come back I liked less."

---

1. **Recognizing Words in Context**

   Find the word *leisurely* in the passage. One definition below is closest to the meaning of that word. One definition has the opposite or nearly the opposite meaning. The remaining definition has a completely different meaning. Label each definition C for *closest*, O for *opposite or nearly opposite,* or D for *different.*

   _____ a. brutally

   _____ b. calmly

   _____ c. frantically

2. **Keeping Events in Order**

   Number each statement below 1, 2, or 3 to show the order in which the events took place.

   _____ a. Nevada enters the corner store.

   _____ b. Nevada walks down the road.

   _____ c. Mr. Jones peers into Nevada's face.

3. Making Evaluations

Two of the statements below describe things that actually happen or are stated in the passage. The other statement is an evaluation, or a judgment or opinion, about a character, setting, or event in the passage. Label each statement E for *evaluation* or H for *happens or is stated in the passage.*

_____ a. Mr. Jones has never sold liquor.

_____ b. Mr. Jones is an honorable man.

_____ c. Mr. Jones recognizes Nevada.

4. Making Correct Inferences

Two of the statements below are correct inferences, or reasonable guesses. They are based on information in the passage. The other statement is an incorrect, or faulty, inference. Label each statement C for *correct* inference or F for *faulty* inference.

_____ a. Before he came into town, Nevada was out on the range.

_____ b. Mr. Jones dislikes Nevada.

_____ c. Nevada has been in this town in the past.

5. Summarizing

One of the statements below is a summary that tells the most important ideas in the passage. The other two statements contain details from the passage. They do not tell the most important ideas in the passage. Label each statement S for *summary* or D for *details.*

_____ a. Nevada returns to Lineville and visits a storekeeper he knows.

_____ b. Nevada comes to a narrow block where people pass to and fro.

_____ c. The corner store smells of merchandise, groceries, and tobacco.

Correct Answers, Part A _____

Correct Answers, Part B _____

Total Correct Answers _____

from **Marriage á la Mode**
by Katherine Mansfield

On his way to the station Williams remembered with a fresh pang of disappointment that he was taking nothing down to the kiddies. Poor little chaps! It was hard on them. Their first words always were as they ran to greet him, "What have you got for me, daddy?" and he had nothing. He would have to buy them some sweets at the station. But that was what he had done for the past four Saturdays. Their faces had fallen last time when they saw the same old boxes again.

And Paddy had said, "I had red ribbing on mine bee-fore!"

And Johnny had said, "It's always pink on mine. I hate pink!"

But what was William to do? The affair wasn't so easily settled. In the old days, of course, he would have taken a taxi off to a decent toy shop and chosen them something in five minutes. But nowadays they had Russian toys, French toys, Serbian toys—toys from God knows where. It was over a year since Isabel had scrapped the old donkeys and engines and so on because they were "so bad for the babies' sense of form."

"It's so important," the new Isabel had explained, "that they should like the right things from the very beginning. It saves so much time later on. Really, if the poor pets have to spend their infant years staring at these horrors, they'll grow up asking to be taken to the Royal Academy."

And she spoke as though a visit to the Royal Academy was certain death to anyone.

"Well, I don't know," said William slowly. "When I was their age I used to go to bed hugging an old towel with a knot in it."

The new Isabel looked at him, her eyes narrowed, her lips apart.

"*Dear* William! I'm sure you did!" She laughed in the new way.

Sweets it would have to be, however, thought William gloomily. He fished in his pocket for change for the taximan. And he saw the kiddies handing the boxes round—they were awfully generous little chaps—while Isabel's precious friends didn't hesitate to help themselves.

What about fruit? William hovered before a stall just inside the station. What about a melon each? Would they have to share that, too? Or a pineapple for Pad, and a melon for Johnny? Isabel's friends could hardly go sneaking up to the nursery at the children's mealtimes.

Reading Time _____

Recalling Facts

1. Paddy and Johnny are tired of receiving
   - ❏ a. fruit.
   - ❏ b. sweets.
   - ❏ c. toys.

2. Johnny doesn't like
   - ❏ a. blue ribbing.
   - ❏ b. red ribbing.
   - ❏ c. pink ribbing.

3. Isabel has thrown out the boys'
   - ❏ a. sweets and fruit.
   - ❏ b. Russian and Serbian toys.
   - ❏ c. old donkeys and engines.

4. When William was a boy, he went to bed with an old
   - ❏ a. towel.
   - ❏ b. donkey.
   - ❏ c. train.

5. At the station, William considers buying the boys
   - ❏ a. a ride in a taxicab.
   - ❏ b. new sweaters.
   - ❏ c. fruit.

Understanding the Passage

6. William does not want to disappoint
   - ❏ a. Isabel's friends.
   - ❏ b. Paddy and Johnny.
   - ❏ c. the stationmaster.

7. In the old days, William
   - ❏ a. never worked on a Saturday.
   - ❏ b. didn't have money to buy presents.
   - ❏ c. had no trouble picking out toys for his sons.

8. The new Isabel scorns
   - ❏ a. fruits and vegetables.
   - ❏ b. all foreign toys.
   - ❏ c. the Royal Academy.

9. William thinks Isabel's friends are
   - ❏ a. cold and distant.
   - ❏ b. simply delightful.
   - ❏ c. a bit rude and greedy.

10. William wants to buy the boys something they will
    - ❏ a. use as adults.
    - ❏ b. take to bed with them.
    - ❏ c. not have to share with Isabel's friends.

14 B   *from* **The Wolves of Cernogratz**
by H. H. Munro

"What is disturbing the animals?" asked the Baron.

And then the humans, listening intently, heard the sound that had roused the dogs to their fear and rage.

"Wolves!" cried the Baron.

Their music broke forth in one raging burst, seeming to come from everywhere.

"Hundreds of wolves," said the Hamburg merchant.

Moved by some impulse which she could not have explained, the Baroness left her guests. She made her way to the narrow, cheerless room where the old governess lay. In spite of the biting cold of the winter night, the window stood open. The Baroness rushed forward to close it.

"Leave it open," said the old woman in a voice that for all its weakness carried an air of command such as the Baroness had never heard before from her lips.

"But you will die of cold!" she said.

"I am dying in any case," said the voice, "and I want to hear their music. They have come from far and wide to sing the death music of my family. It is beautiful that they have come. I am the last Von Cernogratz that will die in our old castle. They have come to sing to me."

1. **Recognizing Words in Context**

   Find the word *intently* in the passage. One definition below is closest to the meaning of that word. One definition has the opposite or nearly the opposite meaning. The remaining definition has a completely different meaning. Label each definition C for *closest*, O for *opposite or nearly opposite*, or D for *different*.

   _____ a. carefully

   _____ b. gradually

   _____ c. lazily

2. **Keeping Events in Order**

   Number each statement below 1, 2, or 3 to show the order in which the events took place.

   _____ a. The Baroness tries to shut the old governess's window.

   _____ b. The old governess explains why the wolves have come.

   _____ c. The people in the castle hear the howls of hundreds of wolves.

3. Making Evaluations

Two of the statements below describe things that actually happen or are stated in the passage. The other statement is an evaluation, or a judgment or opinion, about a character, setting, or event in the passage. Label each statement E for *evaluation* or H for *happens or is stated in the passage*.

_____ a. The old governess is a determined woman.

_____ b. The Baroness leaves the room where her guests are.

_____ c. The dogs have been roused to fear and rage.

4. Making Correct Inferences

Two of the statements below are correct inferences, or reasonable guesses. They are based on information in the passage. The other statement is an incorrect, or faulty, inference. Label each statement C for *correct* inference or F for *faulty* inference.

_____ a. The old governess is alarmed by the presence of the wolves.

_____ b. The humans are surprised that wolves are the source of the disturbance.

_____ c. The Baroness is concerned about the health of the governess.

5. Summarizing

One of the statements below is a summary that tells the most important ideas in the passage. The other two statements contain details from the passage. They do not tell the most important ideas in the passage. Label each statement S for *summary* or D for *details*.

_____ a. The humans listen intently to figure out the source of the sound.

_____ b. The old governess is staying in a cheerless room with an open window.

_____ c. The people hear the singing of wolves as the old governess lies dying.

Correct Answers, Part A _____

Correct Answers, Part B _____

Total Correct Answers _____

from **Victory**
by Joseph Conrad

Heyst and Lena, walking rather fast, approached Wang's hut. He asked the girl to wait. Then Heyst climbed the ladder of bamboos giving access to the door. It was as he had thought. The smoky room was empty, except for a big chest of sandalwood too heavy for hurried removal. Its lid was thrown up. But whatever it might have contained was no longer there. All Wang's things were gone. Without tarrying in the hut, Heyst came back to the girl, who asked no questions, with her strange air of knowing everything.

"Let us push on," he said.

He went ahead, the rustle of her white skirt following him into the shades of the forest, along the path of their usual walk. Twice Heyst looked over his shoulder at her. Behind the readiness of her smile there was a fund of devoted love. They passed the spot where it was their practice to turn towards the barren summit of the central hill. Heyst held steadily on his way towards the upper limit of the forest. The moment they left its shelter, a breeze enveloped them. A great cloud, racing over the sun, threw a somber tint over everything. Heyst pointed up a steep rugged path clinging to the side of the hill. It ended in a barricade of felled trees, a primitive obstacle which must have cost much labor to erect at just that spot.

"This," Heyst explained in his urbane tone, "is a barrier against the march of progress. The poor folk over there did not like it. It appeared to them in the shape of my company—a great step forward, as some people used to call it with mistaken faith. The advanced foot has been drawn back, but the barricade remains."

They went on climbing slowly. The cloud had driven over, leaving an added brightness on the face of the world.

"It's a very ridiculous thing," Heyst went on; "but then it is the product of honest fear—fear of the unknown. It's pathetic, too, in a way. And I wish, Lena, that we were on the other side of it."

"Oh, stop, stop!" she cried, seizing his arm.

The face of the barricade they were approaching had been piled up with a lot of fresh-cut branches. The leaves were still green.

"You had better let me go forward alone, Lena," said Heyst.

Reading Time _____

Recalling Facts

1. Wang's hut is empty except for a
   - ❑ a. big chest.
   - ❑ b. mirror.
   - ❑ c. bed.

2. When Heyst returns from the hut, Lena
   - ❑ a. urges him to push on.
   - ❑ b. asks no questions.
   - ❑ c. wants to know what he found.

3. Lena is wearing
   - ❑ a. jungle clothes.
   - ❑ b. a white skirt.
   - ❑ c. high-heeled shoes.

4. The path Heyst and Lena travel is
   - ❑ a. flat and broad.
   - ❑ b. muddy and dangerous.
   - ❑ c. steep and rugged.

5. The path ends
   - ❑ a. at a cliff.
   - ❑ b. in a barricade of trees.
   - ❑ c. at the river's edge.

Understanding the Passage

6. When Heyst looks inside Wang's hut, he is
   - ❑ a. not surprised.
   - ❑ b. very irritated.
   - ❑ c. intensely shocked.

7. Apparently, Wang
   - ❑ a. was planning to leave.
   - ❑ b. left in a hurry.
   - ❑ c. will be right back.

8. The summit of the central hill is
   - ❑ a. heavily populated.
   - ❑ b. covered with jungle growth.
   - ❑ c. without many trees or vegetation.

9. The barricade is a protest against
   - ❑ a. poor living conditions.
   - ❑ b. the neighboring village.
   - ❑ c. advancing civilization.

10. The barricade has recently been
    - ❑ a. strengthened.
    - ❑ b. removed.
    - ❑ c. abandoned.

from **Alibi Ike**

by Ring Lardner

"What do you think of Alibi Ike?" ast Carey.

"Who's that?" I says.

"This here Farrell in the outfield," says Carey.

"He looks like he could hit," I says.

"Yes," said Carey, "but he can't hit near as good as he can apologize." Then Carey went on to tell me what Ike had been pullin' out there. He'd dropped the first fly ball that was hit to him and told Carey his glove wasn't broke in yet, and Carey says the glove could easy of been Kid Gleason's gran'father. He made a whale of a catch out o' the next one and Carey says "Nice work!" but Ike says he could of caught the ball with his back turned only he slipped when he started after it.

"I thought you done well to get to the ball," says Carey.

"I ought to been settin' under it," says Ike.

"What did you hit last year?" Carey ast him.

"I had malaria most of the season," says Ike. "I wound up with 356."

"Where would I have to go to get malaria?" says Carey, but Ike didn't wise up.

I and Carey and him set at the same table together for supper. It took him half an hour longer'n us to eat because he had to excuse himself every time he lifted his fork.

1. **Recognizing Words in Context**

   Find the phrase *wise up* in the passage. One definition below is closest to the meaning of that word. One definition has the opposite or nearly the opposite meaning. The remaining definition has a completely different meaning. Label each definition C for *closest,* O for *opposite or nearly opposite,* or D for *different.*

   _____ a. study

   _____ b. catch on

   _____ c. misunderstand

2. **Keeping Events in Order**

   Number each statement below 1, 2, or 3 to show the order in which the events took place.

   _____ a. Carey, the narrator, and Ike all eat dinner together.

   _____ b. Ike makes a good catch but says he should have done better.

   _____ c. Carey asks the narrator what he thinks about Ike.

3. Making Evaluations

Two of the statements below describe things that actually happen or are stated in the passage. The other statement is an evaluation, or a judgment or opinion, about a character, setting, or event in the passage. Label each statement E for *evaluation* or H for *happens or is stated in the passage*.

_____ a. Ike is really quite proud of his baseball abilities.

_____ b. Ike takes longer to eat than Carey or the narrator.

_____ c. Ike tells Carey that his glove isn't broken in yet.

4. Making Correct Inferences

Two of the statements below are correct inferences, or reasonable guesses. They are based on information in the passage. The other statement is an incorrect, or faulty, inference. Label each statement C for *correct* inference or F for *faulty* inference.

_____ a. Ike wants people to believe that he is talented.

_____ b. Carey feels sorry for Ike because he hit 356.

_____ c. Carey is somewhat annoyed by Ike's excuses.

5. Summarizing

One of the statements below is a summary that tells the most important ideas in the passage. The other two statements contain details from the passage. They do not tell the most important ideas in the passage. Label each statement S for *summary* or D for *details*.

_____ a. When Ike drops a ball, he tells Carey that his glove isn't broken in.

_____ b. Carey tells the narrator about all the excuses Ike makes.

_____ c. It takes Ike a long time to eat because he pauses to excuse himself.

Correct Answers, Part A _____

Correct Answers, Part B _____

Total Correct Answers _____

16 A   *from* **Sons and Lovers**

by D. H. Lawrence

"By the way," said Dr. Ansell one evening when Morel was in Sheffield, "we've got a man in the fever hospital here who comes from Nottingham— Dawes. He doesn't seem to have many belongings in the world."

"Baxter Dawes!" Paul exclaimed.

"That's the man—has been a fine fellow, physically, I should think. Been in a bit of a mess lately—you know him?"

"He used to work at the place where I am."

"Did he? Do you know anything about him? He's just skulking, or he'd be a lot better than he is by now."

"I don't know anything of his home circumstances, except that he's separated from his wife and has been a bit down, I believe. But tell him about me, will you? Tell him I'll come and see him."

The next time Morel saw the doctor he said:

"And what about Dawes?"

"I said to him," answered the other, "'Do you know a man from Nottingham named Morel?' and he looked at me as if he'd jump at my throat. I said: 'I see you know the name; it's Paul Morel.' Then I told him about your saying you would go and see him. 'What does he want?' he said as if you were a policeman."

"And did he say he would see me?" asked Paul.

"He wouldn't say anything—good, bad, or indifferent," replied the doctor.

"Why not?"

"That's what I want to know. There he lies and sulks, day in, day out— can't get a word of information out of him."

"Do you think I might go?" asked Paul.

"You might."

There was a feeling of connection between the rival men, more than ever since they had fought. In a way Morel felt guilty towards the other, and more or less responsible. And being in such a state of soul himself, he felt an almost painful nearness to Dawes, who was suffering and despairing, too. Besides, they had met in a naked extremity of hate, and it was a bond. At any rate, the elemental man in each had met.

He went down to the isolation hospital, with Dr. Ansell's card. The nurse, a healthy young Irishwoman, led him down the ward.

"A visitor to see you," she said.

Dawes looked swiftly with his dark, startled eyes beyond the nurse at Paul. His look was full of fear, mistrust, hate, and misery.

Reading Time _____

Recalling Facts

1. Dawes comes from
   - ❏ a. Sheffield.
   - ❏ b. Nottingham.
   - ❏ c. St. Paul's.

2. Dawes is
   - ❏ a. separated from his wife.
   - ❏ b. recovering from a broken leg.
   - ❏ c. an extremely wealthy man.

3. Dawes is currently staying in
   - ❏ a. a fever hospital.
   - ❏ b. a friend's house.
   - ❏ c. an inn on the outskirts of town.

4. Morel and Dawes
   - ❏ a. are business partners.
   - ❏ b. previously had a fight.
   - ❏ c. are old and close friends.

5. When Dawes sees Morel, his look is full of
   - ❏ a. surprise.
   - ❏ b. fear.
   - ❏ c. joy.

Understanding the Passage

6. Apparently Dawes has been
   - ❏ a. having a streak of bad luck.
   - ❏ b. injured in a train wreck.
   - ❏ c. arrested by the police.

7. When Dawes hears Morel's name, he becomes
   - ❏ a. violent.
   - ❏ b. calm.
   - ❏ c. suspicious.

8. The doctor
   - ❏ a. knows what is troubling Dawes.
   - ❏ b. suggests that Morel stay away.
   - ❏ c. can't figure out what troubles Dawes.

9. The doctor believes Dawes should be
   - ❏ a. improving more quickly.
   - ❏ b. operated on as soon as possible.
   - ❏ c. protected from Morel.

10. Morel feels
    - ❏ a. bitter anger toward Dawes.
    - ❏ b. some sense of guilt about Dawes.
    - ❏ c. shock that Dawes is still alive.

16 B *from* **The Other House**
by Henry James

"I should like to commemorate your birthday," Paul said. He opened the case, and with its lifted lid he held it out to Jean. "It will give me great pleasure if you'll kindly accept this little ornament."

Jean took it from him—she seemed to study it a minute. "Oh, Paul, oh, Paul!"—her protest was as sparing as a caress with the back of the hand.

"I thought you might care for the stone," he said.

"It's a rare and perfect one—it's magnificent."

"Well, Miss Armiger told me you would know." There was a hint of relaxed suspense in Paul's tone.

Still holding the case open, his companion looked at him a moment. "Did *she* kindly select it?"

He stammered, coloring a little. "No; mother and I did. We went up to London for it; we had the mounting designed and worked out. They took two months. But I showed it to Miss Armiger, and she said you'd spot any defect."

"Do you mean," the girl asked, smiling, "that if you had not had her word for that, you would have tried me with something inferior?"

Paul continued very grave. "You know well enough what I mean."

1. **Recognizing Words in Context**

   Find the word *commemorate* in the passage. One definition below is closest to the meaning of that word. One definition has the opposite or nearly the opposite meaning. The remaining definition has a completely different meaning. Label each definition C for *closest,* O for *opposite or nearly opposite,* or D for *different.*

   _____ a. forget

   _____ b. learn about

   _____ c. celebrate

2. **Keeping Events in Order**

   Number each statement below 1, 2, or 3 to show the order in which the events took place.

   _____ a. Paul opens the case and holds it out to Jean.

   _____ b. Paul shows the stone to Miss Armiger.

   _____ c. Paul and his mother go to London.

3. Making Evaluations

Two of the statements below describe things that actually happen or are stated in the passage. The other statement is an evaluation, or a judgment or opinion, about a character, setting, or event in the passage. Label each statement E for *evaluation* or H for *happens or is stated in the passage.*

_____ a. Jean is very lucky to get such a nice gift.

_____ b. Jean tells Paul that the stone is rare and perfect.

_____ c. Paul blushes when Jean asks if Miss Armiger selected the stone.

4. Making Correct Inferences

Two of the statements below are correct inferences, or reasonable guesses. They are based on information in the passage. The other statement is an incorrect, or faulty, inference. Label each statement C for *correct* inference or F for *faulty* inference.

_____ a. Paul wants his gift for Jean to be perfect.

_____ b. The mounting of the stone is unique and of high quality.

_____ c. Jean is upset that Paul asked Miss Armiger about the stone.

5. Summarizing

One of the statements below is a summary that tells the most important ideas in the passage. The other two statements contain details from the passage. They do not tell the most important ideas in the passage. Label each statement S for *summary* or D for *details.*

_____ a. Paul gives Jean a stone that he has made sure is perfect.

_____ b. Miss Armiger has told Paul that Jean can spot defects in stones.

_____ c. It took two months for the mounting to be designed and worked out.

Correct Answers, Part A _____

Correct Answers, Part B _____

Total Correct Answers _____

from **The Picture of Dorian Gray**
by Oscar Wilde

"What is this all about?" cried Dorian, flinging himself down on the sofa. "I hope it is not about myself. I am tired of myself tonight. I should like to be somebody else."

"It is about yourself," answered Hallward, in his grave, deep voice, "and I must say it to you. I shall only keep you half an hour."

Dorian sighed. "Half an hour!" he murmured.

"It is not much to ask of you, Dorian, and it is entirely for your own sake that I am speaking. I think it right that you should know that the most dreadful things are being said against you in London."

"I don't wish to know anything about them. I love scandals about other people, but scandals about myself don't interest me. They have not got the charm of novelty."

"They must interest you, Dorian. Every gentleman is interested in his good name. You don't want people to talk of you as something vile and degraded. Of course you have your position, and your wealth, and all that kind of thing. But position and wealth are not everything. Mind you, I don't believe these rumors at all. At least, I can't believe them when I see you. Sin is a thing that writes itself across a man's face. It cannot be concealed. People talk sometimes of secret vices. There are no such things. If a wretched man has a vice, it shows itself in the lines of his mouth, the droop of his eyelids, the molding of his hands even. Somebody—I won't mention his name, but you know him—came to me last year to have a portrait done. I had never seen him before, and had never heard anything about him at the time, though I have heard a good deal since. He offered an extravagant price. I refused him. There was something in the shape of his fingers that I hated. I know now that I was quite right in what I fancied about him. His life is dreadful. But you, Dorian, with your pure, bright, innocent face, and your marvelous untroubled youth—I can't believe anything against you. And yet I see you very seldom, and you never come down to the studio now, and when I am away from you, and I heard all these hideous things that people are whispering about you, I don't know what to say."

Reading Time _____

Recalling Facts

1. Hallward has heard
   - ❑ a. good things about Dorian.
   - ❑ b. nasty things about Dorian.
   - ❑ c. nothing about Dorian.

2. Dorian does not want to hear rumors about
   - ❑ a. his brother.
   - ❑ b. his friends.
   - ❑ c. himself.

3. Hallward believes that no man can
   - ❑ a. conceal his vices.
   - ❑ b. understand love.
   - ❑ c. be happy living alone.

4. Dorian has not recently been
   - ❑ a. to London.
   - ❑ b. to Hallward's studio.
   - ❑ c. home.

5. Hallward refuses to paint a man's portrait because he does not like the
   - ❑ a. man's family.
   - ❑ b. shape of the man's fingers.
   - ❑ c. reputation of the man.

Understanding the Passage

6. Hallward's intention is to
   - ❑ a. help Dorian.
   - ❑ b. anger Dorian.
   - ❑ c. confuse Dorian.

7. Apparently, Dorian is
   - ❑ a. an old man.
   - ❑ b. a blind man.
   - ❑ c. a rich man.

8. Hallward does not want to
   - ❑ a. see Dorian.
   - ❑ b. believe the rumors he had heard.
   - ❑ c. leave Dorian alone even for a minute.

9. Hallward believes that Dorian has a
   - ❑ a. guilty look about him.
   - ❑ b. look of complete innocence.
   - ❑ c. dazed and confused look.

10. Dorian does not seem to care
    - ❑ a. how long Hallward will stay.
    - ❑ b. what other people think of him.
    - ❑ c. both a and b.

17 | B | *from* **Dracula**
by Bram Stoker

The old man motioned me in with his right hand with a courtly gesture, saying in excellent English, but with a strange intonation:

"Welcome to my house! Enter freely and of your own will!" He made no motion of stepping to meet me, but stood like a statue. It was as though his gesture of welcome had fixed him into stone. The instant, however, that I had stepped over the threshold, he moved impulsively forward, and holding out his hand grasped mine with a strength which made me wince. The effect was not lessened by the fact that it seemed as cold as ice—more like the hand of a dead than a living man. Again he said:

"Welcome to my house. Come freely. Go safely; and leave something of the happiness you bring!" The strength of the handshake was so much akin to that which I had noticed in the driver, whose face I had not seen, that for a moment I doubted if it were not the same person to whom I was speaking. To make sure, I said:

"Count Dracula?" He bowed in a courtly way as he replied:

"I am Dracula."

1. **Recognizing Words in Context**

   Find the word *courtly* in the passage. One definition below is closest to the meaning of that word. One definition has the opposite or nearly the opposite meaning. The remaining definition has a completely different meaning. Label each definition C for *closest*, O for *opposite or nearly opposite*, or D for *different*.

   _____ a. rude

   _____ b. polite

   _____ c. unusual

2. **Keeping Events in Order**

   Number each statement below 1, 2, or 3 to show the order in which the events took place.

   _____ a. Dracula tells the narrator to enter of his own free will.

   _____ b. The narrator wonders if Dracula is the driver.

   _____ c. Dracula grasps the narrator's hand with a strong grip.

3. Making Evaluations

Two of the statements below describe things that actually happen or are stated in the passage. The other statement is an evaluation, or a judgment or opinion, about a character, setting, or event in the passage. Label each statement E for *evaluation* or H for *happens or is stated in the passage.*

_____ a. Dracula has a strong handshake.

_____ b. The narrator is a brave person.

_____ c. The narrator steps over the threshold.

4. Making Correct Inferences

Two of the statements below are correct inferences, or reasonable guesses. They are based on information in the passage. The other statement is an incorrect, or faulty, inference. Label each statement C for *correct* inference or F for *faulty* inference.

_____ a. Dracula is also the driver.

_____ b. Dracula is pleased to have a visitor.

_____ c. The narrator has never met Dracula before.

5. Summarizing

One of the statements below is a summary that tells the most important ideas in the passage. The other two statements contain details from the passage. They do not tell the most important ideas in the passage. Label each statement S for *summary* or D for *details.*

_____ a. Dracula tells the narrator to enter of his own free will.

_____ b. The narrator enters Dracula's home and notices odd things about him.

_____ c. Dracula moves forward and holds out his hand to the narrator.

Correct Answers, Part A _____

Correct Answers, Part B _____

Total Correct Answers _____

by Stephen Crane

At nightfall the column broke into regimental pieces, and the fragments went into the fields to camp. Tents sprang up like strange plants. Camp fires, like red, peculiar blossoms, dotted the night. The youth kept from intercourse with his companions as much as circumstances would allow him. In the evening he wandered a few paces into the gloom. From this little distance the many fires, with the black forms of men passing to and fro before the crimson rays, made weird and satanic effects.

He lay down in the grass. The blades pressed tenderly against his cheek. The moon had been lighted and was hung in a treetop. The liquid stillness of the night enveloping him made him feel vast pity for himself. There was a caress in the soft winds; and the whole mood of the darkness, he thought, was one of sympathy for himself in his distress.

He wished that he was at home again making the endless rounds from the house to the barn, from the barn to the fields, from the fields to the barn, from the barn to the house. He remembered he had often cursed the brindle cow and her mates, and had sometimes flung milking stools. But, from his present point of view, there was a halo of happiness about each of their heads, and he would have sacrificed all the brass buttons on the continent to have been enabled to return to them. He told himself that he was not formed for a solider. And he mused seriously upon the radical differences between himself and those men who were dodging imp-like around the fires. As he mused thus he heard the rustle of grass. Upon turning his head, he discovered the loud soldier. He called out, "Oh, Wilson!"

The latter approached and looked down. "Why, hello, Henry; is it you? What you doing here?"

"Oh, thinking," said the youth.

The other sat down and carefully lighted his pipe. "You're getting blue, my boy. You're looking thundering peeked. What the dickens is wrong with you?"

"Oh, nothing," said the youth.

The loud soldier launched then into the subject of the anticipated fight. "Oh, we've got 'em now!" As he spoke his boyish face was wreathed in a gleeful smile, and his voice had an exultant ring. "We've got 'em now. By the eternal thunders, we'll lick 'em good!"

Reading Time _____

Recalling Facts

1. The men in the regiment sleep
   - ❏ a. in barracks.
   - ❏ b. deep in the woods.
   - ❏ c. in tents.

2. The youth tries
   - ❏ a. not to talk to the other men.
   - ❏ b. to warm himself by a campfire.
   - ❏ c. to run away.

3. The night is
   - ❏ a. cloudy.
   - ❏ b. rainy.
   - ❏ c. moonlit.

4. At one time the youth had cursed
   - ❏ a. his parents.
   - ❏ b. his cows.
   - ❏ c. brass buttons.

5. The youth's name is
   - ❏ a. Wilson.
   - ❏ b. Henry.
   - ❏ c. not mentioned.

Understanding the Passage

6. The youth feels that he
   - ❏ a. can't wait for the next battle.
   - ❏ b. is fighting on the wrong side.
   - ❏ c. is in a very sad state.

7. The youth wants nothing more than to
   - ❏ a. return to his farm.
   - ❏ b. talk to his friends.
   - ❏ c. fall asleep on the grass.

8. The youth is convinced that he is not cut out for
   - ❏ a. a military career.
   - ❏ b. farming.
   - ❏ c. sleeping in a tent.

9. When the loud soldier arrives, the youth
   - ❏ a. talks without stopping.
   - ❏ b. gives short answers.
   - ❏ c. ignores him.

10. The loud soldier boasts about the upcoming
    - ❏ a. battle.
    - ❏ b. peace treaty.
    - ❏ c. promotion.

18   B   *from* **How It Happened**

by Arthur Conan Doyle

I got along very well until I came to Claystall Hill. It is one of the worst hills in England, a mile and a half long, with three fairly sharp curves. My park gates stand at the very foot of it upon the main London road.

    We were just over the brow of this hill, where the grade is steepest, when the trouble began. I had been on the top speed, and wanted to get it on the free; but it stuck between gears, and I had to get it back on the top again. By this time it was going at a great rate, so I clapped on both brakes. One after the other they gave way. I didn't mind so much when I felt my footbrake snap, but when I put all my weight on my side brake, and the lever clanged to its full limit without a catch, it brought a cold sweat out of me. By this time we were fairly tearing down the slope. The lights were brilliant, and I brought it round the first curve all right. Then we did the second one, though it was a close shave for the ditch.

1. **Recognizing Words in Context**

   Find the word *tearing* in the passage. One definition below is closest to the meaning of that word. One definition has the opposite or nearly the opposite meaning. The remaining definition has a completely different meaning. Label each definition C for *closest*, O for *opposite or nearly opposite*, or D for *different*.

   _____ a. holding

   _____ b. rushing

   _____ c. slowing

2. **Keeping Events in Order**

   Number each statement below 1, 2, or 3 to show the order in which the events took place.

   _____ a. Both brakes give way one after the other.

   _____ b. The narrator drives over the brow of Claystall Hill.

   _____ c. The narrator breaks out in a cold sweat.

3. Making Evaluations

Two of the statements below describe things that actually happen or are stated in the passage. The other statement is an evaluation, or a judgment or opinion, about a character, setting, or event in the passage. Label each statement E for *evaluation* or H for *happens or is stated in the passage.*

_____ a. Claystall Hill is one of the worst hills in England.

_____ b. The trouble begins where the grade of the hill is steepest.

_____ c. The narrator is in a dangerous situation.

4. Making Correct Inferences

Two of the statements below are correct inferences, or reasonable guesses. They are based on information in the passage. The other statement is an incorrect, or faulty, inference. Label each statement C for *correct* inference or F for *faulty* inference.

_____ a. Claystall Hill is difficult to drive even without car problems.

_____ b. The narrator is unfamiliar with the area where he is driving.

_____ c. If the side brake had worked, the situation would have been less dangerous.

5. Summarizing

One of the statements below is a summary that tells the most important ideas in the passage. The other two statements contain details from the passage. They do not tell the most important ideas in the passage. Label each statement S for *summary* or D for *details.*

_____ a. The narrator wants to lower his speed, but the car gets stuck between gears.

_____ b. Claystall Hill is a mile and a half long and has three sharp curves.

_____ c. The narrator's car problems cause a scary drive down Claystall Hill.

Correct Answers, Part A _____

Correct Answers, Part B _____

Total Correct Answers _____

from A Chaparral Christmas Gift
by O. Henry

"Now, boys," said Lane, "keep your eyes open. Walk around the house and watch the road well. All of you know McRoy, or the 'Frio Kid,' as they call him now. If you see him, open fire without asking any questions. I'm not afraid of his coming, but Rosita is. She's been afraid he'd come in on us every Christmas since we were married."

The evening went along nicely. The guests praised Rosita's fine supper. Afterward the men scattered in groups about the rooms.

The Christmas tree, of course, delighted the youngsters. But most of all they were pleased when Santa Claus himself in flowing white beard and furs appeared and began to give out the toys.

"It's my papa," said Billy Sampson, aged six. "I've seen him wear 'em before."

Berkly, a sheepman, an old friend of Lane, stopped Rosita as she was passing by him on the gallery, where he was sitting smoking.

"Well, Mrs. Lane," said he, "I suppose by this Christmas you've gotten over being afraid of that fellow McRoy, haven't you? Madison and I have talked about it, you know."

"Very nearly," said Rosita, smiling, "but I am still nervous sometimes. I shall never forget the awful time when he came so near to killing us."

"He's the most cold-hearted villain in the world," said Berkly. "The citizens all along the border ought to turn out and hunt him down like a wolf."

"He has committed awful crimes," said Rosita, "but—I—don't—know. I think there is a spot of good somewhere in everybody. He was not always bad—that I know."

Rosita turned into the hallway between the rooms. Santa Claus, in muffling whiskers and furs, was just coming through.

"I heard what you said through the window, Mrs. Lane," he said. "I was just going down in my pocket for a Christmas present for your husband. But I've left one for you, instead. It's in the room to your right."

"Oh, thank you, kind Santa Claus," said Rosita, brightly.

She went into the room, while Santa Claus stepped into the cooler air of the yard.

She found no one in the room but Madison.

"Where is my present that Santa said he left for me?" she asked.

"Haven't seen anything in the way of a present," said her husband, laughing, "unless he could have meant me."

Reading Time _____

Recalling Facts

1. Lane tells the men to keep a close watch for
   - ❏ a. Rosita.
   - ❏ b. Billy Sampson.
   - ❏ c. McRoy.

2. The guests praise Rosita for her fine
   - ❏ a. supper.
   - ❏ b. presents.
   - ❏ c. linen.

3. Billy Sampson thinks Santa Claus is
   - ❏ a. his father.
   - ❏ b. the "Frio Kid."
   - ❏ c. Mr. Lane.

4. Santa Claus tells Rosita that her Christmas present is
   - ❏ a. under the tree.
   - ❏ b. near the fireplace.
   - ❏ c. in the room to her right.

5. Madison tells Rosita that
   - ❏ a. Santa Claus has left.
   - ❏ b. he knows of no present.
   - ❏ c. someone has seen the "Frio Kid."

Understanding the Passage

6. The "Frio Kid" is
   - ❏ a. a dinner guest.
   - ❏ b. a sheepman.
   - ❏ c. an outlaw.

7. Rosita is apparently a good
   - ❏ a. gunfighter.
   - ❏ b. cook.
   - ❏ c. storyteller.

8. Rosita believes that
   - ❏ a. no one is completely bad.
   - ❏ b. her fears are unreasonable.
   - ❏ c. the "Frio Kid" is nearby.

9. Santa Claus does not give
   - ❏ a. any gifts to the children.
   - ❏ b. Rosita's husband a present.
   - ❏ c. both a and b.

10. Rosita was
    - ❏ a. a childhood friend of the "Frio Kid."
    - ❏ b. almost killed by the "Frio Kid."
    - ❏ c. present when the "Frio Kid" robbed several banks.

19 | B | *from* **Little Men**

by Louisa May Alcott

"You cannot be too careful; watch your tongue, and eyes and hands, for it is easy to tell, and look, and act untruth," said Mr. Bhaer, in one of the talks he had with Nat.

"I know it, and I don't mean to, but it's so much easier to get along if you ain't very fussy about being exactly true. I used to tell 'em because I was afraid of father and Nicolo. Now I do sometimes because the boys laugh at me. I know it's bad, but I forget," and Nat looked much depressed by his sins.

"When I was a little lad I used to tell lies! Ach! what fibs they were, and my old grandmother cured me of it—how, do you think? My parents had talked, and cried, and punished, but still did I forget as you. Then said the dear old grandmother, 'I shall help you to remember, and put a check on this unruly part,' with that she drew out my tongue and snipped the end with her scissors till the blood ran. That was terrible, you may believe, but it did me much good, because it was sore for days, and every word I said came so slowly that I had time to think."

1. **Recognizing Words in Context**

    Find the word *unruly* in the passage. One definition below is closest to the meaning of that word. One definition has the opposite or nearly the opposite meaning. The remaining definition has a completely different meaning. Label each definition C for *closest*, O for *opposite or nearly opposite*, or D for *different*.

    _____ a. disobedient

    _____ b. well behaved

    _____ c. unwanted

2. **Keeping Events in Order**

    Number each statement below 1, 2, or 3 to show the order in which the events took place.

    _____ a. Mr. Bhaer's parents cry because of his habit of telling lies.

    _____ b. Mr. Bhaer talks with Nat and tells him to watch his tongue.

    _____ c. Nat tells lies because some of the boys laugh at him.

3. Making Evaluations

Two of the statements below describe things that actually happen or are stated in the passage. The other statement is an evaluation, or a judgment or opinion, about a character, setting, or event in the passage. Label each statement E for *evaluation* or H for *happens or is stated in the passage.*

_____ a. Nat once told lies because he was afraid of his father.

_____ b. Mr. Bhaer's grandmother was harsh but wise.

_____ c. Mr. Bhaer tells Nat that he cannot be too careful.

4. Making Correct Inferences

Two of the statements below are correct inferences, or reasonable guesses. They are based on information in the passage. The other statement is an incorrect, or faulty, inference. Label each statement C for *correct* inference or F for *faulty* inference.

_____ a. Nat and Mr. Bhaer have had other talks before.

_____ b. Mr. Bhaer is thankful for what his grandmother did.

_____ c. Nat believes that it is okay to tell lies sometimes.

5. Summarizing

One of the statements below is a summary that tells the most important ideas in the passage. The other two statements contain details from the passage. They do not tell the most important ideas in the passage. Label each statement S for *summary* or D for *details.*

_____ a. Mr. Bhaer talks with Nat and tells how his grandmother helped him stop lying.

_____ b. Nat tells Mr. Bhaer that sometimes the other boys laugh at him.

_____ c. Mr. Bhaer's parents were unable to stop him from lying.

Correct Answers, Part A _____

Correct Answers, Part B _____

Total Correct Answers _____

from **The Lion's Share**
by Arnold Bennett

"I'm unhappy, Miss Ingate," said Audrey. "Now if I wanted to make the best marmalade you ever tasted in your born days, first of all there would be a fearful row about the oranges. Secondly father would tell mother she must tell me exactly what I was to do. He would also tell cook. Thirdly and lastly, dear friends, he would come into the kitchen himself. It wouldn't be my marmalade at all. I should only be a marmalade-making machine. They never let me have any responsibility—not even when mother's operation was on—and I am never truly free. The kitchen maid has far more responsibility than I have, and she has an evening off and an afternoon off. She can write a letter without everybody asking her who she's writing to. She's only seventeen, but she has money and she buys her own clothes. She's a very naughty, wicked girl, and I wish I was in her place. She scorns me, naturally—who wouldn't?"

Miss Ingate said nothing. She merely sat with her hands in the lap of her pale blue dress, faintly and sadly smiling. Audrey burst out, "Miss Ingate, what can I do? I must do something—but what?"

Miss Ingate shook her head, and put her lips tightly together, while smoothing the sides of her grey coat. "I don't know," she said.

"Then *I'll* tell you what I can do!" answered Audrey firmly, wriggling nearer to her along the floor. "And what I definitely shall do. Will you promise to keep it a secret?"

"Yes," Miss Ingate nodded. She smiled, showing her teeth. Her broad polished forehead shone with kindly eagerness.

"Will you swear?"

Miss Ingate hesitated. Then she nodded again.

"Then put your hand on my head and say, 'I swear.'"

Miss Ingate obeyed.

"I shall leave this house," said Audrey in a low voice.

"You won't, Audrey!"

"I'll eat my hand off if I've not left this house by tomorrow."

"Tomorrow!" Miss Ingate practically screamed. "Now, Audrey, do reflect a minute. Think what you are!"

Audrey bounded to her feet.

"That's what father is always saying," she exploded angrily. "He is always telling me to examine myself. The fact is I know too much about myself. I know exactly the kind of girl it is who's going to leave this house. Exactly!"

"Audrey, you frighten me. Where are you going to?"

"London."

Reading Time _____

Recalling Facts

1. Audrey is
   - ❏ a. unhappy.
   - ❏ b. excited.
   - ❏ c. tired.

2. The kitchen maid is
   - ❏ a. fifteen.
   - ❏ b. seventeen.
   - ❏ c. nineteen.

3. Miss Ingate promises to
   - ❏ a. lend Audrey money.
   - ❏ b. speak to the kitchen maid.
   - ❏ c. keep Audrey's secret.

4. Audrey plans to leave
   - ❏ a. in a month.
   - ❏ b. in a week.
   - ❏ c. the next day.

5. Audrey's father often tells Audrey to
   - ❏ a. stop complaining.
   - ❏ b. make marmalade.
   - ❏ c. examine herself.

Understanding the Passage

6. Audrey plans to
   - ❏ a. confront her father.
   - ❏ b. meet with the kitchen maid.
   - ❏ c. run away from home.

7. Audrey feels she needs
   - ❏ a. a more loving mother.
   - ❏ b. more freedom.
   - ❏ c. help making marmalade.

8. Audrey envies
   - ❏ a. her father.
   - ❏ b. Miss Ingate.
   - ❏ c. the kitchen maid.

9. When she hears Audrey's plan, Miss Ingate is
   - ❏ a. delighted.
   - ❏ b. uninterested.
   - ❏ c. distressed.

10. Audrey is
    - ❏ a. determined to leave.
    - ❏ b. comforted by Miss Ingate.
    - ❏ c. furious at the kitchen maid.

20 B *from* **The Ice Maiden**

by Hans Christian Andersen

The hunters reached at length the precipitous ridge of rock. It became even darker here, for the walls of rock almost met, and light penetrated only a little way down from the open space above. Close by, under them, was a deep abyss, with its hoarse-sounding, raging water.

They sat all three quite still. They had to await the dawn of day, when the parent eagle should fly out. Only then could they shoot it if they had any hope to capture the young one. Rudy sat as still as if he had been a portion of the rock on which he sat. He held his gun ready to fire. His eyes were steadily fixed on the highest part of the cleft, under a projecting rock on which the eagle's nest was concealed. The three hunters had long to wait.

At length, high above them was heard a crashing, whirring noise. The air was darkened by a large object soaring in it. Two guns were ready to aim at the enormous eagle the moment it flew from its nest. A shot was fired. For an instant the outspread wings fluttered. Then the bird began to sink slowly and it seemed as if with its size and the stretch of its wings it would fill the whole chasm.

1. **Recognizing Words in Context**

   Find the word *concealed* in the passage. One definition below is closest to the meaning of that word. One definition has the opposite or nearly the opposite meaning. The remaining definition has a completely different meaning. Label each definition C for *closest,* O for *opposite or nearly opposite,* or D for *different.*

   _____ a. displayed

   _____ b. repaired

   _____ c. hidden

2. **Keeping Events in Order**

   Number each statement below 1, 2, or 3 to show the order in which the events took place.

   _____ a. The hunters wait until the dawn of day.

   _____ b. The eagle sinks slowly into the chasm.

   _____ c. The hunters reach the edge of the ridge.

3. Making Evaluations

Two of the statements below describe things that actually happen or are stated in the passage. The other statement is an evaluation, or a judgment or opinion, about a character, setting, or event in the passage. Label each statement E for *evaluation* or H for *happens or is stated in the passage.*

_____ a. The hunters sit very still.

_____ b. The eagle is enormous.

_____ c. The eagle's death is sad.

4. Making Correct Inferences

Two of the statements below are correct inferences, or reasonable guesses. They are based on information in the passage. The other statement is an incorrect, or faulty, inference. Label each statement C for *correct* inference or F for *faulty* inference.

_____ a. The hunters shoot the eagle because it has caused someone harm.

_____ b. The hunters' trip has been carefully planned.

_____ c. The hunters' main goal is to catch the young eagle.

5. Summarizing

One of the statements below is a summary that tells the most important ideas in the passage. The other two statements contain details from the passage. They do not tell the most important ideas in the passage. Label each statement S for *summary* or D for *details.*

_____ a. Under the place where the hunters sit is an abyss with raging water.

_____ b. Hunters shoot a large eagle so they can capture the young one.

_____ c. Two guns are aimed at the eagle as it flies from its nest.

Correct Answers, Part A _____

Correct Answers, Part B _____

Total Correct Answers _____

from **The Virginian**
by Owen Wister

The Swinton barbecue was over. The fiddles were silent, the steer was
eaten, the barrel emptied, or largely so, and the candles extinguished.
Round the house and sunken fire all movement of guests was quiet.
The families were long departed homeward, and after their hospitable
turbulence, the Swintons slept.

Mr. and Mrs. Westfall drove through the night, and as they neared their
cabin there came from among the bundled wraps a still, small voice.

"Jim," said his wife, "I said Alfred would catch cold."

"Bosh! Lizzie, don't you fret. He's a little more than a yearlin', and of
course he'll snuffle." And James kissed his wife.

"Well, how you can speak of Alfred that way, calling him a yearling, as
if he was a calf, and he just as much your child as mine, I don't see, James
Westfall!"

"Why, what under the sun do you mean?"

"There he goes again! Do hurry up home, Jim. He's got a real strange
cough."

So they hurried home. Soon the nine miles were finished, and good
James was unhitching the horses by his stable lantern, while his wife in the
house hastened to commit their offspring to bed. The traces had dropped,
and each horse marched forward for further unbuckling, when James heard
himself called. Indeed, there was that in his wife's voice which made him
jerk out his pistol as he ran. But it was no bear or intruder—only two
strange children on the bed. His wife was glaring down at them. He sighed
with relief and laid down the pistol.

"Put that on again, James Westfall. You'll need it. Look here!"

"Well, they won't bite. Whose are they? Where've you put ours?"

"Where have I—" Utterance forsook this mother for a moment. "And
you ask me!" she continued. "Ask Lin McLean. Ask him that sets bulls
on folks and steals slippers, what he's done with our innocent lambs,
mixing them up with other people's coughing, unhealthy brats. That's
Charlie Taylor in Alfred's clothes, and I know Alfred didn't cough like
that, and I said to you it was strange; and the other one that's been put in
Christopher's new quilts is not even a bub—bub—boy!"

As this crime against society loomed clear to James Westfall's mind, he
sat down on the nearest piece of furniture, and heedless of his wife's tears
and his exchanged children, broke into wild laughter.

Reading Time _____

Recalling Facts

1. Mr. and Mrs. Westfall live in a
   - ❏ a. tent.
   - ❏ b. cabin.
   - ❏ c. hut.

2. Jim calls Alfred a
   - ❏ a. yearling.
   - ❏ b. calf.
   - ❏ c. baby.

3. To get home from the barbecue, the Westfalls have to travel
   - ❏ a. two miles.
   - ❏ b. four miles.
   - ❏ c. nine miles.

4. James comes running with his pistol drawn when he hears
   - ❏ a. his wife's voice.
   - ❏ b. the growl of a bear.
   - ❏ c. the sounds of children crying.

5. James's reaction to the news of the exchanged children is to
   - ❏ a. strap on his gun.
   - ❏ b. laugh.
   - ❏ c. cry.

Understanding the Passage

6. On the way home, the child's coughing
   - ❏ a. doesn't seem to bother Jim.
   - ❏ b. proves that the child isn't Alfred.
   - ❏ c. frightens his parents.

7. The children must be
   - ❏ a. very hungry.
   - ❏ b. upset by the long ride.
   - ❏ c. bundled up from head to toe.

8. As Lizzie starts to put the two children to bed, she
   - ❏ a. asks them to say their prayers.
   - ❏ b. gets them some warm milk.
   - ❏ c. discovers something shocking.

9. Lizzie believes that the person responsible for the prank is
   - ❏ a. Charlie Taylor.
   - ❏ b. Lin McLean.
   - ❏ c. Christopher.

10. The Westfalls' children are
    - ❏ a. both girls.
    - ❏ b. a boy and a girl.
    - ❏ c. both boys.

21 | B | *from* **The Queen of Hearts**
by Wilkie Collins

I opened the door and could see nobody. I dried my tears and looked all
round the room—it was empty. I ran upstairs again to Uncle George's
garret bedroom—he was not there. His cheap hairbrush and old cast-off
razor case that had belonged to my grandfather were not on the dressing
table. Had he got some other bedroom? I went out on the landing, and
called softly, with terror and sinking at my heart—

"Uncle George!"

Nobody answered; but my aunt came hastily up the garret stairs.

"Hush!" she said. "You must never say that name out here again!"

She stopped suddenly and looked as if her own words had frightened her.

"Is Uncle George dead?" I asked.

My aunt turned red and pale, and stammered.

I did not wait to hear what she said. I brushed past her, down the stairs.
My heart was bursting—my flesh felt cold. I ran breathlessly and recklessly
into the room where my father and mother had received me. They were
both sitting there still. I ran up to them, wringing my hands, and crying out
in a passion of tears,

"Is Uncle George dead?"

1. **Recognizing Words in Context**

   Find the word *hastily* in the passage.
   One definition below is closest to
   the meaning of that word. One
   definition has the opposite or nearly
   the opposite meaning. The remaining
   definition has a completely different
   meaning. Label each definition C for
   closest, O for *opposite or nearly opposite*,
   or D for *different*.

   _____ a. slowly

   _____ b. quickly

   _____ c. awkwardly

2. **Keeping Events in Order**

   Number each statement below 1, 2,
   or 3 to show the order in which the
   events took place.

   _____ a. The narrator runs up to
   his parents in a passion of
   tears.

   _____ b. The narrator runs upstairs
   to Uncle George's
   bedroom.

   _____ c. The aunt comes hastily up
   the garret stairs.

3. **Making Evaluations**

   Two of the statements below describe things that actually happen or are stated in the passage. The other statement is an evaluation, or a judgment or opinion, about a character, setting, or event in the passage. Label each statement E for *evaluation* or H for *happens or is stated in the passage.*

   _____ a. The narrator's love for his Uncle George is very moving.

   _____ b. The aunt looks frightened by her own words.

   _____ c. The narrator's flesh feels cold.

4. **Making Correct Inferences**

   Two of the statements below are correct inferences, or reasonable guesses. They are based on information in the passage. The other statement is an incorrect, or faulty, inference. Label each statement C for *correct* inference or F for *faulty* inference.

   _____ a. There is something the narrator doesn't know about Uncle George.

   _____ b. Something bad has happened to Uncle George.

   _____ c. The aunt doesn't know what happened to Uncle George.

5. **Summarizing**

   One of the statements below is a summary that tells the most important ideas in the passage. The other two statements contain details from the passage. They do not tell the most important ideas in the passage. Label each statement S for *summary* or D for *details.*

   _____ a. The narrator's Uncle George is missing, and he is told not to mention him.

   _____ b. Uncle George's cheap hairbrush and old razor case are not on his table.

   _____ c. The aunt stammers when the narrator asks her if Uncle George is dead.

Correct Answers, Part A _____

Correct Answers, Part B _____

Total Correct Answers _____

from **In a German Pension**

by Katherine Mansfield

"Max, you silly devil, you'll break your neck if you go careering down the slide that way. Drop it, and come to the Club House with me and get some coffee."

"I've had enough for today. I'm damp all through. There, give us a cigarette, Victor, old man. When are you going home?"

"Not for another hour. It's fine this afternoon, and I'm getting into decent shape. Look out, get off the track; here comes Fraulein Winkel. Damned elegant the way she manages her sled!"

"I'm cold all through. That's the worst of this place—the mists—it's a damp cold. Here, Foreman, look after this sled—and stick it somewhere so that I can get it without looking through a hundred and fifty others tomorrow morning."

They sat down at a small round table near the stove and ordered coffee. Victor sprawled in his chair, patting his little brown dog Bobo and looking, half laughingly, at Max.

"What's the matter, my dear? Isn't the world being nice and pretty?"

"I want my coffee, and I want to put my feet into my pocket—they're like stones. . . . Nothing to eat, thanks—the cake is like underdone india rubber here."

Fuchs and Wistuba came and sat at their table. Max half turned his back and stretched his feet out to the oven. The three other men all began talking at once—of the weather—of the record slide—of the fine condition of the Wald See for skating. Suddenly Fuchs looked at Max, raised his eyebrows and nodded across to Victor, who shook his head.

"Max doesn't feel well," he said, feeding the brown dog with broken lumps of sugar, "and nobody's to disturb him—I'm nurse."

"That's the first time I've ever known him off color," said Wistuba. "I've always imagined he had the better part of this world that could not be taken away from him. I think he says his prayers to the dear Lord for having spared him being taken home in seven basketsful tonight. It's a fool's game to risk your all that way and leave the nation desolate."

"Dry up," said Max. "You ought to be wheeled about on the snow in a baby carriage."

"Oh, no offense, I hope. Don't get nasty. . . . How's your wife, Victor?"

"She's not at all well. She hurt her head coming down the slide with Max on Sunday."

Reading Time _____

Recalling Facts

1. Max asks Victor for
   - ❏ a. some coffee.
   - ❏ b. a cigarette.
   - ❏ c. a sled.

2. Max asks to have
   - ❏ a. his sled waxed.
   - ❏ b. his sled stored.
   - ❏ c. Fuchs buy more cigarettes.

3. Bobo is the name of
   - ❏ a. a dog.
   - ❏ b. a sled.
   - ❏ c. anyone who fell off a sled.

4. The Wald See is a place for
   - ❏ a. eating.
   - ❏ b. smoking.
   - ❏ c. skating.

5. Victor's wife hurt her head sledding with
   - ❏ a. Fuchs.
   - ❏ b. Wistuba.
   - ❏ c. Max.

Understanding the Passage

6. Victor considers Max's sledding to be
   - ❏ a. rather dangerous.
   - ❏ b. a lot of harmless fun.
   - ❏ c. too expensive.

7. It appears that Max
   - ❏ a. enjoys the damp, cold weather.
   - ❏ b. had trouble finding his sled.
   - ❏ c. wants to slide longer.

8. After Max stops sledding, he feels
   - ❏ a. tired but happy.
   - ❏ b. like getting more exercise.
   - ❏ c. cold and miserable.

9. The other three men
   - ❏ a. praise Max.
   - ❏ b. do not know Max.
   - ❏ c. tease Max.

10. The other three men do not share Max's love for
    - ❏ a. taking risks.
    - ❏ b. coffee and cigarettes.
    - ❏ c. the Wald See.

from The House of Pride
by Jack London

With war guns and rifles, police and soldiers, they came for him, and he was only one man, a crippled wreck of a man at that. They offered a thousand dollars for him, dead or alive. In all his life he had never possessed that much money. The thought was a bitter one. Kapahei had been right. He, Koolau, had done no wrong. Because the whites wanted labor with which to work the stolen land, they had brought in the Chinese coolies, and with them had come the sickness. And now, because he had caught the sickness, he was worth a thousand dollars—but not to himself. It was his worthless carcass, rotten with disease or dead from a bursting shell, that was worth all that money.

When the soldiers reached the knife-edged passage, he was prompted to warn them. But his gaze fell upon the body of the murdered maid, and he kept silent. When six had ventured on the knife edge, he opened fire. Nor did he cease when the knife edge was bare. He emptied his magazine, reloaded, and emptied it again. He kept on shooting. All his wrongs were blazing in his brain, and he was in a fury of vengeance.

1. Recognizing Words in Context

Find the word *ventured* in the passage. One definition below is closest to the meaning of that word. One definition has the opposite or nearly the opposite meaning. The remaining definition has a completely different meaning. Label each definition C for *closest*, O for *opposite or nearly opposite*, or D for *different*.

_____ a. gone out

_____ b. pulled back

_____ c. covered up

2. Keeping Events in Order

Number each statement below 1, 2, or 3 to show the order in which the events took place.

_____ a. Koolau shoots the soldiers on the knife-edged passage.

_____ b. Police and soldiers come for Koolau with guns and rifles.

_____ c. The whites bring in Chinese people to work the land.

3. **Making Evaluations**

Two of the statements below describe things that actually happen or are stated in the passage. The other statement is an evaluation, or a judgment or opinion, about a character, setting, or event in the passage. Label each statement E for *evaluation* or H for *happens or is stated in the passage.*

_____ a. Koolau is worth one thousand dollars dead or alive.

_____ b. It is unfortunate that Koolau has caught the sickness.

_____ c. The soldiers are shot in a fury of vengeance.

4. **Making Correct Inferences**

Two of the statements below are correct inferences, or reasonable guesses. They are based on information in the passage. The other statement is an incorrect, or faulty, inference. Label each statement C for *correct* inference or F for *faulty* inference.

_____ a. Koolau plans to surrender to the soldiers but changes his mind.

_____ b. Koolau believes the whites do not have the right to use the land.

_____ c. Koolau has never been a wealthy man.

5. **Summarizing**

One of the statements below is a summary that tells the most important ideas in the passage. The other two statements contain details from the passage. They do not tell the most important ideas in the passage. Label each statement S for *summary* or D for *details.*

_____ a. Koolau empties his magazine, reloads it, and keeps shooting.

_____ b. Because Koolau has caught the sickness, he is worth one thousand dollars.

_____ c. Koolau, who is ill, shoots at the soldiers who are coming for him.

Correct Answers, Part A _____

Correct Answers, Part B _____

Total Correct Answers _____

from **The Maker of Moons**

by Robert W. Chambers

"Have you ever drawn a picture of a corpse?" asked Jamison next morning as I walked into his private room with a sketch of the proposed full page of the Zoo.

"No, and I don't want to," I replied, sullenly.

"Let me see your Central Park page," said Jamison in his gentle voice. I displayed it for him. It was worthless as a work of art but it pleased Jamison. I knew that it would.

"Can you finish it by this afternoon?" he asked.

"Oh, I suppose so," I said, wearily. "Anything else, Mr. Jamison?"

"The corpse," he replied. "I want a sketch by tomorrow—finished."

"What corpse?" I demanded, controlling myself as I met Jamison's soft eyes.

There was a mute duel of glances. Jamison passed his hand across his forehead with a slight lifting of the eyebrows.

"I shall want it as soon as possible," he said.

"Where is this corpse?" I asked.

"In the morgue—have you read the morning papers? No? Ah—as you very rightly observe you are too busy to read the morning papers. Young men must learn industry first, of course. What you are to do is this: the San Francisco police have sent out an alarm regarding the disappearance of a Miss Tufft—the millionaire's daughter, you know. Today a body was brought to the morgue here in New York. It has been identified as the missing young lady—by a diamond ring. Now I am sure that it isn't, and I'll show you why."

He picked up a pen and made a sketch of a ring on a margin of that morning's *Tribune*.

"That is the description of her ring as sent on from San Francisco. You notice the diamond is set in the center of the ring where the two gold serpents' *tails* cross!"

"Now the ring on the finger of the woman in the morgue is like this," and he rapidly sketched another ring where the diamond rested in the *fangs* of the two gold serpents.

"That is the difference," he said in his pleasant, even voice.

"Rings like that are common," said I. I then remembered that I had seen such a ring on the finger of the white-faced girl in the Park the evening before. Then a sudden thought took shape—perhaps that was the girl whose body lay in the morgue!

Reading Time _____

Recalling Facts

1. The narrator has just completed his
   sketch of the
   - ❑ a. Zoo.
   - ❑ b. morgue.
   - ❑ c. ring.

2. Jamison wants the narrator to draw a
   picture of
   - ❑ a. an ill person.
   - ❑ b. an accident.
   - ❑ c. a corpse.

3. Miss Tufft is the daughter of a
   - ❑ a. gem dealer.
   - ❑ b. millionaire.
   - ❑ c. politician.

4. The missing young lady was
   identified by her
   - ❑ a. clothing.
   - ❑ b. dental records.
   - ❑ c. diamond ring.

5. Jamison's remarks make the narrator
   remember the girl he had seen
   - ❑ a. many years ago.
   - ❑ b. early last year.
   - ❑ c. the evening before.

Understanding the Passage

6. Jamison appears to be the narrator's
   - ❑ a. best friend.
   - ❑ b. boss.
   - ❑ c. attorney.

7. Jamison wants the narrator to
   - ❑ a. work quickly.
   - ❑ b. help the young girl.
   - ❑ c. get him the morning papers.

8. Miss Tufft's hometown is
   - ❑ a. New York.
   - ❑ b. San Francisco.
   - ❑ c. Chicago.

9. Jamison believes that the police
   - ❑ a. are on the right track.
   - ❑ b. are working much too slowly.
   - ❑ c. have incorrectly identified the
     corpse.

10. The narrator
    - ❑ a. thinks he might have seen the
      dead woman before.
    - ❑ b. shows little interest in
      Jamison's idea.
    - ❑ c. knows how the young lady died.

23 B *from* **The Posthumous Papers of the Pickwick Club**

by Charles Dickens

"I knew that she could not live long, but the thought that before her death she might give birth to some ill-fated being, destined to hand down madness to its offspring, determined me. I resolved to kill her.

"For many weeks I thought of poison, and then of drowning, and then of fire. A fine sight the grand house in flames, and the madman's wife smouldering away to cinders. I thought often of this, but I gave it up at last. Oh! the pleasure of stropping the razor day after day, feeling the sharp edge, and thinking of the gash one stroke of its thin bright edge would make!

"At last the old spirits who had been with me so often before whispered in my ear that the time was come, and thrust the open razor into my hand. I grasped it firmly, rose softly from the bed, and leaned over my sleeping wife. Her face was buried in her hands. I withdrew them softly, and they fell listlessly on her bosom. She had been weeping; for the traces of the tears were still wet upon her cheek. Her face was calm; and even as I looked upon it, a tranquil smile lighted up her pale features.

1. **Recognizing Words in Context**

   Find the word *tranquil* in the passage. One definition below is closest to the meaning of that word. One definition has the opposite or nearly the opposite meaning. The remaining definition has a completely different meaning. Label each definition C for *closest*, O for *opposite or nearly opposite*, or D for *different*.

   _____ a. peaceful

   _____ b. grateful

   _____ c. anxious

2. **Keeping Events in Order**

   Number each statement below 1, 2, or 3 to show the order in which the events took place.

   _____ a. The narrator resolves that he will kill his wife.

   _____ b. The narrator moves his sleeping wife's hands.

   _____ c. The narrator feels the sharp razor blade each day.

3. Making Evaluations

Two of the statements below describe things that actually happen or are stated in the passage. The other statement is an evaluation, or a judgment or opinion, about a character, setting, or event in the passage. Label each statement E for *evaluation* or H for *happens or is stated in the passage.*

_____ a. The narrator's wife is asleep.

_____ b. The narrator is planning to kill his wife.

_____ c. The narrator's wife is to be pitied.

4. Making Correct Inferences

Two of the statements below are correct inferences, or reasonable guesses. They are based on information in the passage. The other statement is an incorrect, or faulty, inference. Label each statement C for *correct* inference or F for *faulty* inference.

_____ a. The narrator's wife is unhappy.

_____ b. The narrator is afraid of his wife.

_____ c. The narrator hears voices.

5. Summarizing

One of the statements below is a summary that tells the most important ideas in the passage. The other two statements contain details from the passage. They do not tell the most important ideas in the passage. Label each statement S for *summary* or D for *details.*

_____ a. The narrator considers using poison, drowning, and fire.

_____ b. The narrator plans to kill his dying wife before she can pass his madness on to a child.

_____ c. The narrator's wife has been weeping but is now calmly asleep in her bed.

Correct Answers, Part A _____

Correct Answers, Part B _____

Total Correct Answers _____

24   A   *from* The Old Woman in the Wood

by The Brothers Grimm

A poor servant-girl was once traveling with the family with which she
was in service through a great forest. When they were in the midst of it,
robbers came out of the thicket, and murdered all they found. All perished
together except the girl, who had jumped out of the carriage in a fright,
and hidden herself behind a tree. When the robbers had gone away with
their booty, she came out and beheld the great disaster. Then she began to
weep bitterly. She cried, "What can a poor girl like me do now? I do not
know how to get out of the forest. No human being lives in it, so I must
certainly starve." She walked about and looked for a road, but could find
none. When it was evening she seated herself under a tree, gave herself into
God's keeping, and resolved to sit waiting there and not go away, no matter
what happened. When, however, she had sat there for a while, a white dove
came flying to her with a little golden key in its mouth. It put the little key
in her hand, and said, "Do you see that great tree? Therein is a little lock;
it opens with the tiny key, and there you will find food enough, and suffer
no more hunger." The girl went to the tree and opened it. She found milk
in a little dish and white bread to break into it, so that she could eat her
fill. When she was satisfied, she said, "It is now the time when the hens at
home go to roost. I am so tired I could go to bed too." Then the dove
flew to her again. It brought another golden key in its bill, and said, "Open
that tree there, and you will find a bed." So she opened it. She found a
beautiful white bed and she prayed God to protect her during the night.
She lay down and slept. In the morning the dove came for the third time. It
again brought a little key and said, "Open that tree there, and you will find
clothes." And when she opened it, she found garments beset with gold and
with jewels, more splendid than those of any king's daughter. So she lived
there for some time. The dove came every day and provided her with all she
needed.

Reading Time _____

Recalling Facts

1. The robbers attack the family
   - ❏ a. in the great forest.
   - ❏ b. along a town road.
   - ❏ c. near the coast.

2. The girl hides herself behind
   - ❏ a. the carriage.
   - ❏ b. a rock.
   - ❏ c. a tree.

3. The key carried by the white dove is
   - ❏ a. silver.
   - ❏ b. golden.
   - ❏ c. wooden.

4. Inside the first tree the girl finds milk and
   - ❏ a. honey.
   - ❏ b. cookies.
   - ❏ c. bread.

5. The dove comes to see the girl
   - ❏ a. twice.
   - ❏ b. three times.
   - ❏ c. every day.

Understanding the Passage

6. The robbers can best be described as
   - ❏ a. thoughtful.
   - ❏ b. bloodthirsty.
   - ❏ c. bumbling.

7. After viewing the disaster, the girl feels
   - ❏ a. relieved.
   - ❏ b. hopeless.
   - ❏ c. vengeful.

8. The dove knows that the girl
   - ❏ a. is in need.
   - ❏ b. has never been in a forest before.
   - ❏ c. is a friend of the robbers.

9. After a while the girl
   - ❏ a. adjusts to her life in the forest.
   - ❏ b. makes her home with the dove.
   - ❏ c. loses the keys the dove has given her.

10. The dove can best be described as
    - ❏ a. annoying.
    - ❏ b. helpful.
    - ❏ c. sad.

from **Buried Alive**
by Fyodor Dostoyevsky

One night I was on guard. It was in autumn, the wind whistled in the trees, and the night was so dark that I could see nothing at all. I was walking up and down all by myself, and feeling so wretched. I cannot tell you how wretched I was. I took my gun from my shoulder, unscrewed the bayonet, and laid it on the ground. Then I pulled off my right boot, put the muzzle to my breast, leaned heavily on it, pressing down the trigger at the same time with my big toe. It misfired! I examined the gun carefully, cleaned it, loaded it afresh, and again put it to my breast. The powder flashed in the pan, but the gun misfired again. Well, I put on my boot, shouldered my gun, screwed on the bayonet, and again marched up and down. And then I made up my mind to do something desperate only to have done with that wretched life. Half an hour later up comes the colonel at the head of the patrol. What does he do but swear at me for not carrying my gun properly. So I took it in both hands, and stuck the bayonet right into him.

1. **Recognizing Words in Context**

   Find the word *desperate* in the passage. One definition below is closest to the meaning of that word. One definition has the opposite or nearly the opposite meaning. The remaining definition has a completely different meaning. Label each definition C for *closest*, O for *opposite or nearly opposite*, or D for *different*.

   _____ a. ordinary

   _____ b. extreme

   _____ c. incorrect

2. **Keeping Events in Order**

   Number each statement below 1, 2, or 3 to show the order in which the events took place.

   _____ a. The soldier puts his boot back on.

   _____ b. The soldier leans on his gun and presses the trigger.

   _____ c. The soldier stabs the colonel with his bayonet.

3. Making Evaluations

Two of the statements below describe things that actually happen or are stated in the passage. The other statement is an evaluation, or a judgment or opinion, about a character, setting, or event in the passage. Label each statement E for *evaluation* or H for *happens or is stated in the passage*.

_____ a. The soldier is not thinking clearly.

_____ b. The soldier is alone and feels wretched.

_____ c. The soldier gets yelled at by the colonel.

4. Making Correct Inferences

Two of the statements below are correct inferences, or reasonable guesses. They are based on information in the passage. The other statement is an incorrect, or faulty, inference. Label each statement C for *correct* inference or F for *faulty* inference.

_____ a. The bayonet is attached to the soldier's gun.

_____ b. The soldier will do anything to change his situation.

_____ c. The soldier feels respect for the colonel.

5. Summarizing

One of the statements below is a summary that tells the most important ideas in the passage. The other two statements contain details from the passage. They do not tell the most important ideas in the passage. Label each statement S for *summary* or D for *details*.

_____ a. The soldier is on guard at night, and the wind is whistling in the trees.

_____ b. The soldier's gun misfires even after he has examined and cleaned it.

_____ c. The soldier fails to kill himself and then stabs his colonel.

Correct Answers, Part A _____

Correct Answers, Part B _____

Total Correct Answers _____

108

from **The Princess**

by D. H. Lawrence

They scrambled downwards, splashed across stream, up rocks and along the trail of the other side. Romero's black horse stopped, looked down quizzically at the fallen trees, then stepped over lightly. The Princess's sorrel followed, carefully. But Miss Cummins's buckskin made a fuss, and had to be got round.

In the same silence, save for the clinking of the horses and the splashing as the trail crossed stream, they worked their way upwards in the tight, tangled shadow of the canyon.

They were getting fairly high. Then again they dipped and crossed stream, the horses stepping gingerly across a tangle of fallen, frail aspen stems, then suddenly floundering in a mass of rocks. The black emerged ahead, his black tail waving. The Princess let her mare find her own footing; then she too emerged from the clatter. She rode on after the black. Then came a great frantic rattle of the buckskin behind. The Princess was aware of Romero's dark face looking round, with a strange, demonlike watchfulness, before she herself looked round, to see the buckskin scrambling rather lamely beyond the rocks, with one of his pale buff knees already red with blood.

"He almost went down!" called Miss Cummins.

But Romero was already out of the saddle and hastening down the path. He made quiet little noises to the buckskin, and began examining the cut knee.

"Is he hurt?" cried Miss Cummins anxiously, and she climbed hastily down.

"Oh, my goodness!" she cried, as she saw the blood running down the slender buff leg of the horse in a thin trickle. "Isn't that *awful*?" She spoke in a stricken voice, and her face was white.

Romero was still carefully feeling the knee of the buckskin. Then he made him walk a few paces. At last he stood up straight and shook his head. "Not very bad!" he said. "Nothing broken."

Again he bent and worked at the knee. Then he looked up at the Princess. "He can go on," he said. "It's not bad."

"What, go on up here?" cried Miss Cummins. "How many hours?"

"About five," said Romero simply.

"Five hours!" cried Miss Cummins. "A horse with a lame knee! And a steep mountain! Why-y!"

"Yes, it's pretty steep up there," said Romero, pushing back his hat and staring fixedly at the bleeding knee.

Reading Time _____

Recalling Facts

1. Romero is riding a
   - ❏ a. buckskin.
   - ❏ b. sorrel.
   - ❏ c. black horse.

2. The Princess and her companions are traveling
   - ❏ a. through a canyon.
   - ❏ b. along a road.
   - ❏ c. through the desert.

3. The buckskin cuts its
   - ❏ a. knee.
   - ❏ b. neck.
   - ❏ c. nose.

4. Romero says the horse's injury is
   - ❏ a. life threatening.
   - ❏ b. fairly extensive.
   - ❏ c. not serious.

5. Romero estimates that they will not reach their destination for
   - ❏ a. two hours.
   - ❏ b. five hours.
   - ❏ c. eight hours.

Understanding the Passage

6. The buckskin seems quite
   - ❏ a. uncomfortable on the rugged trail.
   - ❏ b. content when off a marked path.
   - ❏ c. nervous around the Princess.

7. The Princess has
   - ❏ a. never ridden a horse before.
   - ❏ b. faith in her horse.
   - ❏ c. great love for Romero.

8. Romero feels that
   - ❏ a. Miss Cummins should turn around and go home.
   - ❏ b. he should put the horse out of its misery.
   - ❏ c. the buckskin will be all right.

9. Miss Cummins's reaction to the horse's injury is one of
   - ❏ a. shame.
   - ❏ b. resignation.
   - ❏ c. horror.

10. Romero believes the journey
    - ❏ a. was well planned.
    - ❏ b. will never end.
    - ❏ c. should continue.

25 B   *from* **A Father**

by Anton Chekhov

"I admit I have had a drop. You must excuse me. I went into a beer shop on the way here, and as it was so hot I had a couple of bottles. It's hot, my boy."

Old Musatov took a shabby rag out of his pocket and wiped his shaven, battered face with it.

"I have come only for a minute, Borenka, my angel," he went on, not looking at his son, "about something very important. Excuse me, perhaps I am hindering you. Haven't you ten rubles, my dear, you could let me have till Tuesday? You see, I ought to have paid for my lodging yesterday, and money, you see! None! Not to save my life!"

Young Musatov went out without a word, and began whispering on the other side of the door with the landlady of the summer villa and his colleagues who had taken the villa with him. Three minutes later he came back, and without a word gave his father a ten-ruble note. The latter thrust it carelessly into his pocket without looking at it, and said:

"Thanks. Well, how are you getting on? It's a long time since we met."

1. **Recognizing Words in Context**

   Find the word *hindering* in the passage. One definition below is closest to the meaning of that word. One definition has the opposite or nearly the opposite meaning. The remaining definition has a completely different meaning. Label each definition C for closest, O for *opposite or nearly opposite*, or D for *different*.

   _____ a. accusing

   _____ b. assisting

   _____ c. bothering

2. **Keeping Events in Order**

   Number each statement below 1, 2, or 3 to show the order in which the events took place.

   _____ a. Old Musatov has a couple of bottles at a beer shop.

   _____ b. Old Musatov asks his son to loan him some money.

   _____ c. Young Musatov whispers with his landlady and colleagues.

3. Making Evaluations

Two of the statements below describe things that actually happen or are stated in the passage. The other statement is an evaluation, or a judgment or opinion, about a character, setting, or event in the passage. Label each statement E for *evaluation* or H for *happens or is stated in the passage.*

_____ a. Old Musatov wipes his face with a rag.

_____ b. Young Musatov gives his father money.

_____ c. Old Musatov takes advantage of his son.

4. Making Correct Inferences

Two of the statements below are correct inferences, or reasonable guesses. They are based on information in the passage. The other statement is an incorrect, or faulty, inference. Label each statement C for *correct* inference or F for *faulty* inference.

_____ a. The father and son do not have a very close relationship.

_____ b. Young Musatov never wants to see his father again.

_____ c. Old Musatov is not good at managing money.

5. Summarizing

One of the statements below is a summary that tells the most important ideas in the passage. The other two statements contain details from the passage. They do not tell the most important ideas in the passage. Label each statement S for *summary* or D for *details.*

_____ a. Young Musatov has taken a villa for the summer, along with some of his colleagues.

_____ b. Old Musatov goes to see his son and gets money from him.

_____ c. Old Musatov goes to a beer shop for a couple of bottles because it is so hot outside.

Correct Answers, Part A _____

Correct Answers, Part B _____

Total Correct Answers _____

ANSWER KEY

READING RATE GRAPH

COMPREHENSION SCORE GRAPH

COMPREHENSION SKILLS PROFILE GRAPH

Answer Key

A	1. b	2. c	3. b	4. a	5. c	6. a	7. a	8. a	9. b	10. a
B	1. C, D, O	2. 2, 3, 1	3. H, E, H	4. F, C, C	5. D, D, S
A	1. b	2. c	3. a	4. c	5. a	6. a	7. b	8. b	9. b	10. b
B	1. D, C, O	2. 1, 3, 2	3. E, H, H	4. C, C, F	5. S, D, D
A	1. c	2. c	3. b	4. a	5. a	6. b	7. a	8. c	9. c	10. b
B	1. C, O, D	2. 3, 2, 1	3. H, H, E	4. C, C, F	5. D, S, D
A	1. a	2. b	3. c	4. c	5. c	6. a	7. c	8. c	9. a	10. c
B	1. O, C, D	2. 3, 1, 2	3. H, E, H	4. C, F, C	5. S, D, D
5A	1. c	2. a	3. b	4. b	5. c	6. b	7. a	8. a	9. c	10. b
5B	1. O, D, C	2. 3, 2, 1	3. E, H, H	4. C, C, F	5. D, S, D
6A	1. c	2. b	3. c	4. b	5. a	6. a	7. b	8. b	9. b	10. b
6B	1. D, O, C	2. 1, 3, 2	3. H, E, H	4. C, F, C	5. S, D, D
A	1. b	2. c	3. a	4. a	5. c	6. a	7. c	8. c	9. c	10. a
B	1. C, O, D	2. 3, 1, 2	3. H, H, E	4. C, C, F	5. D, D, S
A	1. b	2. a	3. c	4. b	5. c	6. a	7. b	8. c	9. c	10. b
B	1. O, C, D	2. 2, 3, 1	3. H, E, H	4. F, C, C	5. D, S, D
9A	1. b	2. b	3. c	4. b	5. c	6. c	7. b	8. a	9. b	10. a
B	1. O, D, C	2. 2, 1, 3	3. E, H, H	4. F, C, C	5. S, D, D
10A	1. c	2. b	3. a	4. b	5. c	6. b	7. b	8. a	9. c	10. a
10B	1. D, C, O	2. 1, 2, 3	3. H, E, H	4. C, C, F	5. D, S, D
11A	1. c	2. c	3. a	4. b	5. b	6. a	7. b	8. b	9. c	10. a
11B	1. C, D, O	2. 2, 1, 3	3. E, H, H	4. C, F, C	5. D, D, S
A	1. c	2. a	3. a	4. c	5. b	6. c	7. a	8. b	9. c	10. a
B	1. C, O, D	2. 2, 2, 1	3. H, H, E	4. F, C, C	5. D, D, S
A	1. c	2. a	3. b	4. b	5. b	6. b	7. a	8. a	9. b	10. b
B	1. D, C, O	2. 2, 1, 3	3. H, E, H	4. C, F, C	5. S, D, D

14A	1. b	2. c	3. c	4. a	5. c	6. b	7. c	8. c	9. c	10. c
14B	1. C, D, O		2. 2, 3, 1		3. E, H, H		4. F, C, C		5. D, D, S	
15A	1. a	2. b	3. b	4. c	5. b	6. a	7. b	8. c	9. c	10. a
15B	1. D, C, O		2. 3, 1, 2		3. E, H, H		4. C, F, C		5. D, S, D	
16A	1. b	2. a	3. a	4. b	5. b	6. a	7. c	8. c	9. a	10. b
16B	1. O, D, C		2. 3, 2, 1		3. E, H, H		4. C, C, F		5. S, D, D	
17A	1. b	2. c	3. a	4. b	5. b	6. a	7. c	8. b	9. b	10. b
17B	1. O, C, D		2. 1, 3, 2		3. H, E, H		4. F, C, C		5. D, S, D	
18A	1. c	2. a	3. c	4. b	5. b	6. c	7. a	8. a	9. b	10. a
18B	1. D, C, O		2. 2, 1, 3		3. H, H, E		4. C, F, C		5. D, D, S	
19A	1. c	2. a	3. a	4. c	5. b	6. c	7. b	8. a	9. b	10. b
19B	1. C, O, D		2. 1, 3, 2		3. H, E, H		4. C, C, F		5. S, D, D	
20A	1. a	2. b	3. c	4. c	5. c	6. c	7. b	8. c	9. c	10. a
20B	1. O, D, C		2. 2, 3, 1		3. H, H, E		4. F, C, C		5. D, S, D	
21A	1. b	2. a	3. c	4. a	5. b	6. a	7. c	8. c	9. b	10. c
21B	1. O, C, D		2. 3, 1, 2		3. E, H, H		4. C, C, F		5. S, D, D	
22A	1. b	2. b	3. a	4. c	5. c	6. a	7. b	8. c	9. c	10. a
22B	1. C, O, D		2. 3, 2, 1		3. H, E, H		4. F, C, C		5. D, D, S	
23A	1. a	2. c	3. b	4. c	5. c	6. b	7. a	8. b	9. c	10. a
23B	1. C, D, O		2. 1, 3, 2		3. H, H, E		4. C, F, C		5. D, S, D	
24A	1. a	2. c	3. b	4. c	5. c	6. b	7. b	8. a	9. a	10. b
24B	1. O, C, D		2. 2, 1, 3		3. E, H, H		4. C, C, F		5. D, D, S	
25A	1. c	2. a	3. a	4. c	5. b	6. a	7. b	8. c	9. c	10. c
25B	1. D, O, C		2. 1, 2, 3		3. H, H, E		4. C, F, C		5. D, S, D	

READING RATE

Put an X on the line above each lesson number to show your reading time and words-per-minute rate for that lesson.

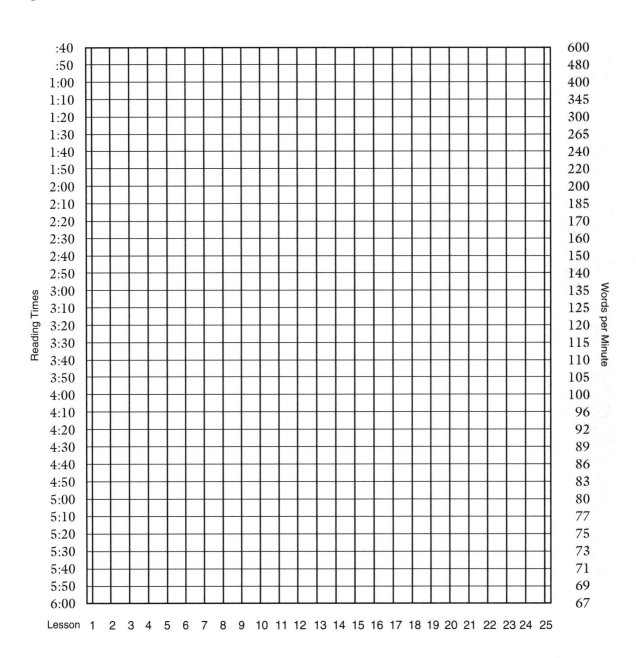

COMPREHENSION SCORE

Put an X on the line above each lesson number to indicate your total correct answers and comprehension score for that lesson.

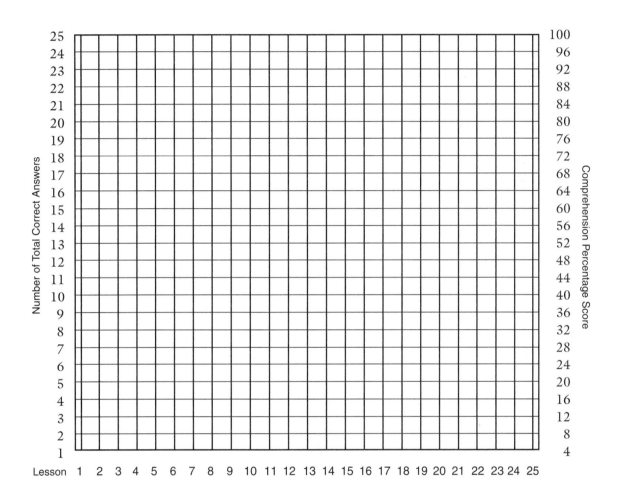

COMPREHENSION SKILLS PROFILE

Put an X in the box above each question type to indicate an incorrect reponse to any question of that type.

Lesson 1					
2					
3					
4					
5					
6					
7					
8					
9					
10					
11					
12					
13					
14					
15					
16					
17					
18					
19					
20					
21					
22					
23					
24					
25					
	Recognizing Words in Context	Keeping Events in Order	Making Evaluations	Making Correct Inferences	Summarizing